40 Shorter Walks

Aviemore

and the

Cairngorms

D1342811

The authors and publisher have made every effort to ensure that the information in this publication is accurate, and accept no responsibility whatsoever for any loss, injury or inconvenience experienced by any person or persons whilst using this book.

published by
pocket mountains ltd
The Old Church, Annanside, Moffat,
Dumfries and Galloway DG10 9HB
pocketmountains.com

ISBN-13: 978-0-9554548-7-5

Extract from *The Cairngorms* by Adam Watson reprinted with kind permission of the Scottish Mountaineering Club (smc.org.uk)

A catalogue record for this book is available from the British Library

Contains Ordnance Survey data © Crown copyright and database right 2018

Printed in Poland. Reprinted 2018

Introduction

The Cairngorms make up Britain's largest National Park. Four of the five highest Scottish mountains rise from a vast wilderness of high plateaux, deep corries and empty glens, a place where only the fittest venture. However, this is encircled by equally stunning landscapes – heather moors, marshes and floodplains, lochs and rivers – within the reach of the average rambler. Most celebrated are the pinewoods – the largest fragments of the great Caledonian forest which once cloaked Scotland. It is hardly surprising that the Cairngorms are unrivalled for wildlife: 25 percent of Britain's most threatened species make their homes here.

The range takes its modern name from Cairn Gorm – the best known, though not the highest, of the summits. But to Gaelic speakers, this is *Am Monadh Ruadh*, 'the Red Hill Range', as distinct from *Am Monadh Liath*, or 'the Grey Hill Range', rising on the other side of the Spey. Cairn Gorm actually means 'Blue Hill'. The confusion is perhaps testament to how the mountain skyline changes its hue as the light shifts each day from dawn to dusk.

This guide features 40 easier walks in all parts of the region, ranging from waymarked rambles to routes exploring the Cairngorms' many hidden corners.

Safety and what to take
While some of the routes are waymarked, many others are not and the sketch maps accompanying them are intended as an aid to planning rather than navigation. It is recommended that you take – and know how to use – the relevant OS or Harvey map and compass.

The Cairngorms experience some of Britain's most extreme weather. The Meall a'Bhuachaille and Coire an t-Sneachda routes, in particular, cross high and exposed ground and, even at lower altitudes, the weather can change rapidly. It is always advisable to carry wind- and waterproof clothing and adequate warm layers to allow the walks to be completed safely if the weather does deteriorate. Most of the routes are suitable for families with children in good conditions and could be completed in stout walking shoes, but boots are recommended for the more exposed or rougher ground.

Access
The northern part of the National Park is served by the mainline railway from Perth to Inverness, and there are good bus services to most towns and villages. Where a walk can be reached by public transport, we have indicated this in the text. Timetables can be found in tourist information centres throughout the region and from Traveline Scotland.

The introduction of the Land Reform (Scotland) Act in 2003 gave walkers rights of access over most of Scotland away from residential buildings, but these rights entail responsibilities. Remember that much of the area is a working landscape, and always follow the Scottish Outdoor Access Code. In particular, keep dogs on tight leads during the spring and early summer and well away from sheep and lambs at all times. This also applies to the pinewoods where even a friendly dog can scare capercaillie and their chicks during the breeding season, as well as affecting many other rare species. Irresponsible dog walkers are a growing problem in some parts of the National Park. Bag and bin dog waste – in open country as well as on paths. It is not acceptable to leave bags hanging on trees or in undergrowth.

Natural history and wildlife

Conservation designations such as Sites of Special Scientific Interest (SSSIs) cover 39 percent of the the park and there are no fewer than eight National Nature Reserves. More than a quarter of Scotland's remnant original forest is in the National Park and provides wonderful opportunities for wildlife- and birdwatching. Species to watch for include the Scottish crossbill, Britain's only endemic bird, and the capercaillie, known to Gaels as 'the Horse of the Woods' although sightings of these are rare. The crested tit is also specific to the pinewoods and a regular visitor to the feeders at Loch an Eilein. Pine martens and wildcats are more elusive, but visitors should watch out for the widespread and almost impossibly cute red squirrels.

The osprey is the symbol of the National Park and probably the species for which the area is best known. Driven to

extinction in Britain in Victorian times, it returned to Loch Garten in the 1950s and can be seen there in spring and summer. There are many other vital habitats here, including the country's largest area of arctic-alpine plateaux and its many rare plant species. This is also a stronghold of the golden eagle and home to the ptarmigan, dotterel and snow bunting. Also deserving special mention are the great salmon rivers of the Spey and Dee, and the Insh Marshes – one of Europe's most important wetland habitats and well-equipped with hides for birdwatchers.

History

For such a wild and remote area, the Cairngorms has much to offer in terms of history. One of the more impressive early remains is the Iron Age hill fort at Dun da-Lamh, while the ruins of historic townships can be seen from the Wildcat Trail and you can visit the reconstruction of Baile Gean at the fascinating Highland Folk Museum by Newtonmore.

Mainstream history exploded into the region with the Jacobite uprisings which followed the exile of King James II of England and VII of Scotland in 1688. The first rising, led by John Graham who defeated the government forces at the Battle of Killiecrankie in 1689, was soon repressed. In the major uprising of 1715, clan leaders were summoned to a great 'hunting match', said to have been at the Punch Bowl by Linn of Quoich. Within days, the Jacobite standard was unfurled near Braemar and soon Aberdeen, Montrose and Inverness were all in the rebels' hands. Following the eventual battle at Sheriffmuir, the Jacobites retreated and the government began the attempt to subdue the Highlands, now seen as a major threat. Sections of one of the roads built under the command of General Wade to connect a series of forts remain – a focal point being the great army barracks at Ruthven, overlooking the Insh Marshes. Wade's efforts did not, however, prevent the second major uprising, led by Bonnie Prince Charlie in 1745. The Jacobites were eventually crushed at Culloden in 1746 and the Highlands repressed ruthlessly. The clan system began to collapse as the remaining chiefs abandoned their role as guardian of their people and began instead to look for profits.

As the cities of southern Britain expanded, demand for food and leather began to rocket and the era of cattle droving reached its peak. Thousands of cattle were driven south annually by drovers, using routes such as the Lairig Ghru as well as the Wade roads: old drove roads feature in many of these walks.

Life took a turn for the worse for the Highlanders when economics shifted the emphasis from cattle to sheep. Townships like Baile Gean were abandoned as chiefs increased rents, clearing out their people to make way for livestock. As with elsewhere in the Highlands, people were forced to turn to emigration. Many of their stories were lost, but one emigration from Badenoch was immortalised in a Gaelic song by Donald Campbell. Those intending to go ascended Creag Bheag (visited on one of the walks) before they began their long journey to Australia.

By the 19th century, field sports became the fashionable pastime amongst Britain's elite: better even than taking part was buying your own estate. The new trend was redoubled when Queen Victoria and Prince Albert bought Balmoral on Deeside. Elaborate shooting-lodges and mansions began to spring up, examples of which are seen on many of the routes.

Rising incomes and the coming of the railway began to bring Highland visits within reach of the ordinary public. Kingussie and Newtonmore expanded to cater for 19th-century visitors, whilst by the 1960s Aviemore was being developed as a purpose-built resort. The village's fortunes declined over the following decades, but it has now taken its place at the centre of the region's expanding tourism industry.

Conservation became an increasingly important priority too. The RSPB bought the Insh Marshes and the Abernethy Forest Estate, whilst the National Trust for Scotland purchased Mar Lodge Estate. National Nature Reserves and other designations were declared to protect parts of the region, and in 2003 the Cairngorms became Scotland's second – and Britain's largest – National Park.

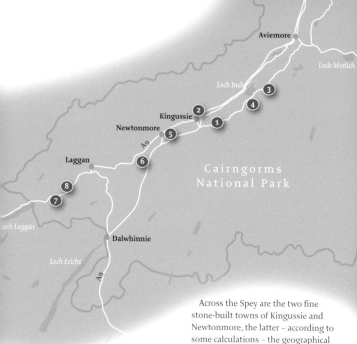

The ancient region of Badenoch, whose name is derived from the Gaelic for 'the drowned land', is the uppermost section of the Spey Valley. The natural floodplains of the river, the Insh Marshes, are recognised internationally as an important wetland site and a remarkable haven for birdlife. Presiding over the marshes are the atmospheric remains of Ruthven Barracks, a reminder of the 1745 Jacobite rebellion and today a great place from which to survey the beauty of the area.

Across the Spey are the two fine stone-built towns of Kingussie and Newtonmore, the latter – according to some calculations – the geographical centre of Scotland. Though only 5km apart, the two towns are divided through their intense rivalry in the Highland sport of shinty, their clubs being the most successful in the history of the game and their matches always a great spectacle.

The lonely Monadhliath is a vast, rolling range of hills shielding the area from the cold north winds, whilst to the south rise the higher and more dramatic peaks of the Cairngorm plateau itself. Higher up the Spey is Laggan, its landscape made familiar through the BBC TV series *Monarch of the Glen*.

Ruthven Barracks ▸

Badenoch

Insh Marshes Invertromie Trail

Distance 4.5km **Time** 2 hours
Terrain obvious path with wooden steps
in places **Map** OS Explorer OL56 **Access** bus
or train to Kingussie 1.5km away

**This meandering trail passes through
attractive birch woodland whilst giving
fine views across the Insh Marshes, one of
Europe's most important wetlands and a
National Nature Reserve owned by the
RSPB. The route visits three hides from
which you can watch the abundant
birdlife in comfort.**

The trail begins at the Insh Marshes
Reserve car park, just off the B970 between
Kingussie and Insh. From here, you can
make your first short detour via a path to
Gordonhall hide before checking out the
impressive double-decker circular Lookout
hide. In spring and summer, waders such
as lapwing, curlew, snipe and redshank can
be spotted, as well as the occasional
feeding osprey.

During autumn and winter, migratory
birds move in and the now flooded
marshes become home to greylag geese,
whooper swans, teal, wigeon and
fieldfares, whilst hen harriers look for easy
pickings. From time to time, the hide is
manned by a ranger, but usually you need
to bring your own binoculars and use the
posters for help with identification.

To start the walk, climb the steps at the
back of the parking area. At the top, there
is a viewpoint where you can scan the
marsh before heading along the trail.
The marshes form the largest area of
floodplain in Britain that has not been
improved or drained, making them vitally
important for conservation. Because the
water level in the marshes is constantly
changing, you'll find the outlook very
different on each visit. Keep to the trail as
it accompanies a fence with woodland on
the left, crossing a small wooden bridge.
Just beyond, there is a chance to detour

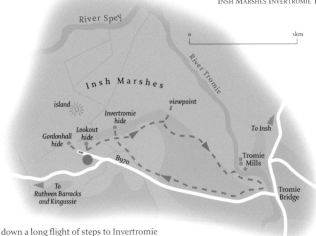

down a long flight of steps to Invertromie hide, which has some of the best views of the wetlands and their birds.

After the junction for the hide, climb gently across grassland towards the woods. Pass through a small gate and continue on the narrow but clear path through the trees. Roe deer are often seen in this area and, in autumn, many species of fungi can be found. Soon, you'll come to a sign indicating another possible detour to a viewpoint with a picnic table.

From the sign, turn right to follow the white arrow markers, continuing by the path to a gate where you cross the track and pick up another path on the far side: this follows a small ridge with good views and lots of purple heather in late summer and autumn. Pass through another gate to enter a birch woodland, carpeted in heavy lichens. Curve to the left downhill and then bear right at the bottom near the River Tromie.

A wall leads you alongside the river to soon pass through a kissing gate and emerge on Tromie Bridge Meadow, part of the RSPB reserve. Follow the riverbank, looking across to Tromie Mills on the far side. Some 150 different plant species have been identified in this meadow alone, and in summer it is a fantastic place to see orchids and butterflies.

The path eventually heads away from the river to a junction. Ignore the green track to the left which leads to a gate onto the B970 near Tromie Bridge; instead, take the path marked with a white arrow in a westerly direction. This passes through woods and grazing land before crossing a track. Traverse another livestock field to reach a gate which brings you back to the path opposite the steps to Invertromie hide. Turn left here and return along the outward route to the car park.

◄ Insh Marshes from Gordonhall hide

Creag Bheag from Kingussie

Distance 7km **Time** 3 hours **Terrain** tracks, paths and open moor (can be wet underfoot); a couple of steep descents **Map** OS Explorer OL56 **Access** Kingussie is well served by buses and trains

An excellent circular walk, starting from the heart of Kingussie to climb past imposing stone villas, through woods and across moorland to the summit of Creag Bheag overlooking the town. The return takes in Tom Baraidh pinewoods – with an excellent chance of spotting red squirrels.

The walk starts in Ardvonie Park near the centre of Kingussie. To reach it from the main street, turn up the road next to the Duke of Gordon Hotel where there is free parking and information on the town's several waymarked walking routes: this excellent varied circuit combines the Creag Bheag and Tom Baraidh routes. Begin by sloping uphill between the information board

and the public toilets to join a road. Turn right up the road and, after a short distance, take the track on the left – signed for West Terrace and Creag Bheag.

The impressive stone villas that you pass were built after the arrival of the railway in 1863, when Kingussie became a popular Highland resort. Originally a tiny hamlet, Kingussie was transformed when the Duke of Gordon began building a new village here in 1799, laying out the wide main street and several fine buildings. The ongoing expansion received a boost when the River Spey was bridged here, putting Kingussie on the main route between Inverness and Perth.

As the track continues, it enters two gates and climbs through woodland (keep to the main route, ignoring any turnings on the left) to eventually emerge on open moor via a small gate. Turn right at the junction, aiming for the summit ridge of Creag Bheag: the crossing of the heather

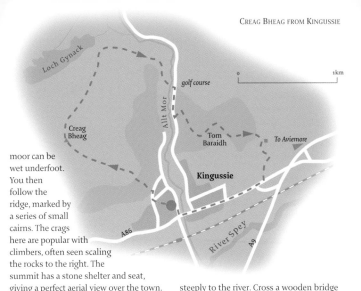

moor can be wet underfoot. You then follow the ridge, marked by a series of small cairns. The crags here are popular with climbers, often seen scaling the rocks to the right. The summit has a stone shelter and seat, giving a perfect aerial view over the town.

Carry on along the path to descend, with views of Loch Gynack, backed by the bare, rolling hills of the Monadhliath. The path becomes much steeper and rougher as it passes some scattered birch trees. At the next junction, you can turn right to return directly to Kingussie or continue straight on, now following signs for the Golf Course Circular. Turn right before Loch Gynack to go through a gate and a section of forestry. The path narrows and emerges from the trees at a bench. Bear left here to reach the ruins of the Toman an t-Seomair township, with Kingussie Golf Club beyond. Pass to the left of the old house to reach an attractive section of path running along a little wooded ridge between the golf course and the riverside.

The path soon bears left and drops very steeply to the river. Cross a wooden bridge and turn right onto a surfaced drive, which leads you through the golf course to a signed junction after 1km. You can carry straight on for a shortcut to Kingussie, but you risk missing one of the route highlights, as the track on the left leads through a gate into woodland that teems with red squirrels. Beyond the gate, go left to join the Tom Baraidh walk.

Keep to the green waymarkers as the path meanders through the pine forest to a four-way wooden signpost near a bench. Turn sharp left, signed for Kingussie, and climb a stile, bearing right through two gates to a winding, stony lane. This passes in front of a large green barn before joining the Kingussie road at the eastern end of town. Turn right to return to the centre of the village.

◀ Kingussie war memorial with Creag Bheag behind

11

Lower Glen Feshie Sculpture Trail

Distance 4.5km **Time** 2 hours
Terrain waymarked paths and tracks
with some ascent **Map** OS Explorer OL57
Access daily bus from Coylumbridge
on schooldays. Car park (charge)
at Feshiebridge

This walk offers the chance to wander
amongst the giant wood and stone
sculptures of the late Frank Bruce before
exploring the peaceful landscape of lower
Glen Feshie. Children will enjoy the
meandering paths and the artworks,
some of which are more than 6m high,
and there are picnic tables near the start
of the walk as well as a beautiful stretch
of riverbank.

The Frank Bruce Sculpture Trail lies just
to the west of Feshiebridge off the B970.

Laid out by the Forestry Commission, the
trail provides an apt setting for the giant
sculptures that Bruce created, many using
timber from the local forest. Bruce found
his inspiration in both landscape and
global politics. There are long-term plans
for an interpretation centre and indoor
exhibition space here but, for now, you
can simply enjoy the works – perhaps at
their best – in this ever-changing, natural
woodland gallery.

To start the walk, follow the waymarked
Sculpture Trail, climbing to the higher
track and turning right before taking the
footpath from the rear of the disabled
parking area. Each of the sculptures is
accompanied by a title and description.
The path wends its way through the
woods, passing *The Archetype*, *The Thinker*

and a huge sculpture called *The Walker*. Soon it comes to the edge of what was once the walled gardens of Invereshie House. Enter the walled area, where you'll find more sculptures as well as good views of the surrounding countryside and tables for a picnic.

Exit the walled garden by a gate in the side wall towards the bottom, and turn left to skirt along the wall by a path. Keep an eye out for a trail, marked by an orange post, on your right. This leads down to the banks of the beautiful River Feshie, where you turn right and walk upstream, crossing a small wooden bridge at one point. After passing the river gauging station, head up the path to return to the car park.

To complete the circuit, leave the car park by the top left-hand corner, just past a telegraph pole, where you'll find a path with a yellow waymarker post. This follows the course of the river and, after passing a picnic table, comes to a lovely stone bridge over the Feshie where the water rushes through a narrow gorge. Cross the road to take the track opposite, passing four houses before arriving in an open area with views of the mountains across the glen.

Carry on along the track as it heads up the glen until you come to a stone wall.

Turn right here to accompany the wall uphill by a path, keeping to the yellow indicators when the path dives into the forest part way up the hill. It emerges from here onto a forest road, which you follow for a short distance before taking a marked path downhill to the right: watch out for mountain bikers who can tear down this path at terrific speed. When you reach the tarmac road, go straight across to join the track leading back down into the car park.

◄ The River Feshie

Uath Lochans and Inshriach Forest

Distance 4km **Time** 1 hour 30
Terrain clear paths and tracks with one
steep climb **Map** OS Explorer OL56
Access no public transport

**This group of four small lochans nestled
amidst the pines of Glen Feshie in the
heart of Inshriach Forest remains a little-
visited treasure. The walk climbs to
Farleitter Crag for wonderful views.**

The route begins from the Forestry
Commission car park and picnic area,
accessed from the forestry road up the
west side of Glen Feshie and signposted
for Uath Lochans. In summer, this
peaceful spot comes to life with water
lilies and dancing dragonflies, making the
tables here a perfect spot for picnics.
Follow the red marker posts to the far side
of the parking area, and turn left onto a
track curving around the first lochan.
Ignoring two paths to the left, continue
straight ahead and begin the steady climb,

keeping right at any further junctions as
you watch for the red markers.

Once the gradient eases off, the route
passes through a stand of fine Scots pine,
some of which are more than 120 years
old. Turn right onto a smaller path which
rises steeply again to reach the top of
Farleitter Crag. The views from here are
magnificent, taking in the lochans, Glen
Feshie and the mountains beyond.

The path keeps to the top of the crag,
coiling round to face the Spey Valley. Here,
a seat next to a large rock provides a
different outlook – over Loch Insh, its
marshes and the River Spey itself to the
rolling hills of the Monadhliath. Follow
the path as it leads away from the edge of
the crag and downhill into the forestry
plantations. Carry straight on ahead,
ignoring a path to the left, to reach a
T-junction: turn right here.

The Badenoch Way soon joins from the
left: this is an 18km linear route running

◄ Uath Lochans from Farleitter Crag

from Ruthven Barracks to Loch Alvie.
When you reach a track, turn right to
follow the trail gently downhill, through
a clearing and along a line of pylons.
The Badenoch Way continues as a path
ahead, but your route keeps to the track
as it bears to the right into the woods.
This stretch gives ample opportunity
for spotting red squirrels as they sprint up
and down the tree trunks: stop still and
listen as they are much easier to identify if
you hear them rustling in the branches
first. At the next junction, turn right and
skirt the edge of the woods.

Keep following the red marker posts and
soon, high above you, Farleitter Crag will
come into view again. The track passes a
more open area before rejoining the
outward route. Turn left here to head back
to the car park.

Newtonmore Wildcat Trail

Distance up to 11km **Time** up to 4 hours
Terrain waymarked paths with some
rougher sections **Map** OS Explorer OL56
Access Newtonmore is well served by
buses and trains

**This circular walk runs right around the
fringes of Newtonmore, taking in a mix of
moor, riverside and native woodland,
with lots of wildlife – though the chances
of spotting the elusive wildcat are slim.**

From the centre of Newtonmore, take
the Perth road and then the first left down
Station Road. Turn right by the first in a
row of railway cottages, a little short of the
station, then left just before the entrance
sign for the Jack Richmond Memorial
Woodland Park. Using the railway crossing
with care, follow the distinctive Wildcat
Trail signs across the field to the River
Spey and turn right. The line of trees

heading straight to a tunnel under the
railway line marks the route of the Coffin
Road, once used to carry the dead to the
Banchor graveyard. The coffins would have
been brought in boats to this point before
the final journey to their resting place.

The path diverts briefly from the water
to avoid a flood-prone area. Pass under the
railway and road to reach the confluence
of the Spey and the Calder, with good
views to craggy Creag Dubh. The well-
marked path now shadows the Calder,
passing through a dense thicket and
diverting around an eroded section before
climbing to the road at Calder Bridge.

On the far side, go left through a gate
and then right after a second gate onto a
riverside path. Beyond the next small gate,
this rises steeply to eventually cross the
steep slopes where the River Calder forces
its way through a lovely wooded gorge.

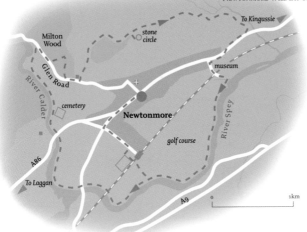

Still waymarked, the path emerges into open country, heading diagonally uphill away from the river. There are stunning views up Glen Banchor with several seats for a break. The great curve of the river gave the glen its name: *Beannachar* is Gaelic for 'a horn-shaped meander'. Turn right onto Glen Road where a marker post indicates a left into the Milton Wood larch plantation. Turn right through a felled area and then left downhill onto Glen Road again. After a small house on the right, take the track signed for Moss Cottage on the left. Pass the buildings and go through a gate with good views to the hills of the Monadhliath. The route now weaves its way through birchwoods and a number of small gates. Look out for a signposted diversion to a Pictish stone circle near the Katie Calder memorial seat.

Beyond the last plantation, go over a footbridge and follow the marker posts left and then right, passing a sheepfank and crossing some grazing land which contains the scant remains of houses from a time when this area was much more heavily populated. Continue through gates to reach the Allt Laraidh Falls. A footbridge crosses the small burn on the right, where you head up the bank and through another gate. The path now keeps company with the Allt Laraidh.

At the main road, turn right. A narrow path runs through the woods, parallel to the road. Opposite the first houses, cross over onto a signed track which passes through sections of the excellent Highland Folk Museum and over the railway bridge. Go through a gate and stay between a fence and a burn, before crossing a footbridge and turning right between the golf course and the Spey. The river leads back to the outward route across the fields from the station.

◀ Creag Dubh above Glen Banchor

The Falls of Truim

Distance 9km **Time** 3 hours **Terrain** paths
and forest tracks; can be muddy
Map OS Explorer OL56
Access no public transport

Visit the Falls of Truim for the chance to
see salmon leaping or canoeists shooting
the rapids. You can either make a very
short circular walk near the falls or follow
the longer route described here, which
takes in open pastures and pleasant
forestry, including an optional climb to a
high crag overlooking the Upper Spey.

The Falls of Truim are just off the A9
south of Newtonmore. Turn off at the sign
for Crubenmore and Dalwhinnie to reach a
car park on the left. From here, walk a
short way back along the road towards the
A9 and take the turning on the left for
Crubenbeg. Very soon, you go through a
kissing gate on the right onto a path
signed for the Falls of Truim. As you
approach the falls themselves, you can
make a detour down to the water –
although there are better views from the
other side of the river. Cross the
roadbridge and take the signed path on
the right to follow the crags above the
falls, where you'll see a fine stand of
Scots pine. The river flows through a
dramatic rocky gorge here, and the falls
are one of the best places in Scotland to
watch salmon leaping – especially in
September and October after heavy rains.

Continue on the path, passing a bench,
as it leaves the river to wander through the
heather. Go through a gate and directly
across a field, turning right at a marker
onto a faint grassy track. Pass through
another gate and beneath Crubenbeg
House, a modern replacement for an old
farmhouse which was destroyed in a fire.
Keep left where the track forks, and then
climb a sometimes muddy ramp beside
Crubenbeg Steading. From here, follow the
clear track diagonally uphill with a fence
on your left.

Go straight across the first field, and

◄ Falls of Truim

pass through a metal gate next to a green right of way sign marked for the Perth road. Turn right along a grassy track, with the stone wall on your right. Glen Truim Woods can be seen up ahead, whilst there are good views across the glen to the western fringes of the Cairngorms.

The track leads you to the woods, entering by a gate. Keep straight ahead, ignoring the turning to the right signed Glen Truim Woods. At the next signed junction, you can detour to the Truim Woods viewpoint by following a marked track off to the left. This takes you up to the top of Creagan an Fhithich – meaning 'the Crag of the Raven' in Gaelic. There is a cairn and bench here, with spectacular views over the wide strath of Badenoch to the Monadhliath mountains beyond. Return the same way to the junction with the forestry track. Turn left to continue through the forest until the track emerges on a minor road.

Here you can make another short detour to the left, this time to visit the Shanvall Memorial, built in honour of Ewan Macpherson who led a group of local men in support of Bonnie Prince Charlie in the 1745 Jacobite uprising.

Otherwise, turn right on reaching the road and carry on along this until you reach a signposted gate and track which dives back into the forest on the right. Follow this, keeping right at the fork to rejoin the outward route.

Now turn left to retrace your steps out of the forest and alongside the wall, eventually returning to the Falls of Truim and the parking area.

Pattack Falls and the lost village

Distance 4.5km Time 1 hour 30
Terrain good paths, forest tracks
Map OS Explorer OL55
Access no public transport

A gentle waymarked walk through a
varied landscape, giving good views of
the waterfalls and gorge on the
River Pattack. The route also includes a
visit to the atmospheric ruins of the
deserted village of Druim an Aird.

Begin from the Druim an Aird car park
on the south side of the A86, between the
village of Laggan and the foot of Loch
Laggan. Take the waymarked path to the
southwest, ignoring a branch off to the
right as you climb uphill to meet a
junction. The viewing platform high above
the Pattack Falls is on the right here. The
falls, which can also be seen from the road,
are particularly impressive after heavy rain,
and the gorge was featured as a location in

the popular TV series *Monarch of the Glen*.

From the falls, continue to climb along
the main upward-trending path, ignoring
the faint trail nearer to the river as it peters
out after a short distance. At a waymarked
junction, turn left to loop through the
attractive pinewoods before bearing south
over more open ground: the dense covering
of heather turns this into a spectacular sea
of purple during late summer and autumn.
A clear path leads downhill to a picnic
bench, completing the loop at a junction.
Turn left here and then left again when you
come to a forestry track, passing a small
house on the right.

Immediately after the house, turn right
onto a footpath signed for Dalwhinnie. The
path follows a water culvert for a short
distance before passing through a gate and
rising slightly: this section can be muddy
underfoot at times. As you climb through
the woodland, you pass a seat carved from

◄ Pattack Falls

a tree trunk and soon arrive at an area of open ground where the trees have been felled to give expansive views of Strath Mashie and the countryside that surrounds it.

Continue straight on, with the fence on your left. The path leads you deeper into the forest and, for a short while, along a firebreak between the pines. Beyond is another clearing, and you'll soon see the remains of Druim an Aird in a fenced enclosure to the left. There is no record of why Druim an Aird was abandoned, but one theory is that the villagers left after their menfolk had died in a snowstorm returning from celebrations at a nearby wedding. These sorry ruins are rapidly becoming part of the landscape itself.

From here, the path takes you to a junction where you turn right along a track. After passing a picnic bench and emerging out into open country with good views ahead, the track descends. Turn right at the next junction and make your way back to the T-junction where you met the forest tracks earlier. Turn left here to climb uphill, keeping left at a fork and crossing the heathery ground before dropping back down into the woodland. Soon you reach the viewing platform for the falls and the path back to the Druim an Aird car park at the start.

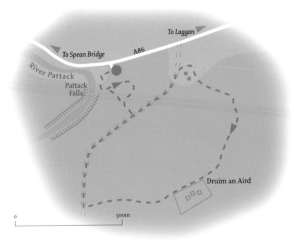

Black Wood and the hill fort

Distance 8.5km **Time** 3 hours
Terrain mostly waymarked paths; steep
Map OS Explorer OL55
Access no public transport

A chance to explore a well-preserved
Pictish hill fort with wonderful views
along Strath Mashie and the surrounding
mountains on the way.

Begin from the car park for Pattack
Falls on the south side of the A86. Cross the
main road and turn left for a very short
time before heading right into an old
parking area with a vehicle barrier.

The start of the walk can be a little hard
to find from here. As you enter the parking
area bear left and then right to find the
start of the initially unmarked route, a
wide green path that descends to pass
through a gap in a fence before rising and
turning right beside the first blue
waymarker post.

After passing an old quarry, the path
eventually emerges from the trees at a

small lochan where you turn left onto
a forestry track.

After a while, you'll spy an optional
detour through the trees to visit the
atmospheric remains of a settlement,
now almost submerged in dense forestry.
The path is wiggly though easy to
navigate, but you do need to retrace
your steps to the main track as the path
that continues past the ruins does not
go to the fort.

As the forestry track continues to rise, a
transmitter mast is clearly visible ahead:
this provides TV reception to Laggan, and
was built after years of campaigning and
fundraising by local residents. Before you
reach the mast, take the signed turn-off
on the left for a steep climb which steers you
left and then right through open country
to attain the ridge with its scattering of
lovely Scots pine.

The path now meanders along the top of
the ridge to the right, soon reaching the
summit, marked by a small cairn. There

◄ Black Craig with Dun da-Lamh on the right

are great views north into the head of the Spey Valley and eastwards over Badenoch towards the Cairngorms range. Continue along the ridge path as it drops steeply into the woods.

Further down, you come to a picnic table and path junction. Turn left uphill if you want to detour through the woodland to the fort of Dun da-Lamh. A diagonally rising path traverses the side of Black Craig and the outer wall of the fort. These remains are impressive for their great age, dating from the earliest Pictish period of around 550BC, and for their almost impregnable position, with the ground falling away for more than 180m on three sides. The external wall is 6m thick and there are also traces of an inner wall. Its Gaelic name means 'Fort of the Two Hands', which is thought to refer either to its dual-facing position or the hill's two small summits.

From the top of the wall, bear right to visit the highest point where you'll find a stone howff or shelter, probably built by the local Home Guard as a fire-watching lookout during the Second World War. The site was well-chosen: it commands a magnificent view in all directions.

Return to the junction at the picnic table, and continue left, signed for Achduchil. This becomes a track, sloping downhill to another junction and picnic table where, this time, you carry straight on by the signpost for Pattack.

A little further on, turn left onto a smaller waymarked path. This passes a bench at the bottom of the wooded section before joining another track through a felled area. Keep going straight ahead, passing the end of the path to the ruined settlement and bearing right at yet another junction. This leads back to the lochan you passed near the start of the walk. Turn left here to head back to the car park and the A86.

Map labels:
Dun-da-Lamh Fort
Strath Mashie
To Laggan
Allt Snìomhach
Black Craig
Black Wood
Strathmashie House
A86
mountain bike centre
ruins
To Spean Bridge
Pattack Falls
River Pattack
0   1km

Strathspey is the stunning central section of the Spey Valley, traditionally stretching from Nethy Bridge to Aviemore. To this side, the Cairngorms present their finest front, extending from mighty Braeriach in the west to Bynack More in the east. This great wall is sculpted by a whole series of dramatic, craggy, ice-carved corries and broken in two by the dark, mysterious cleft of the Lairig Ghru.

Beneath the mountains are Britain's two largest areas of ancient forest – the magnificent Caledonian pinewoods of Abernethy and Rothiemurchus, each encompassing several beautiful lochs. It is little wonder that the area is renowned for its wildlife, from the plentiful red squirrel to the endangered capercaillie.

The town of Aviemore became the heart of the region when it was purpose-built as a skiing and tourist centre in the 1960s. Its architecture soon dated, helping to speed its decline in the 1980s, but with the original Aviemore Centre demolished it has become a lively and thriving resort once more. Nearby villages such as Carrbridge, Boat of Garten and the lovely Nethy Bridge offer alternative centres for those looking for quieter holidays. The whole region offers superb walks for all levels of ability.

Crested tit ▶

Aviemore and Strathspey

Loch Morlich circular

Distance 6km **Time** 1 hour 30
Terrain waymarked trail, almost level
Map OS Explorer OL57 **Access** bus from
Aviemore and Grantown-on-Spey. Car
park (charge) at Glenmore

Loch Morlich has one of Scotland's finest
settings. Fringed by beaches and forest,
its crowning glory is the stunning
backdrop of the often snow-powdered
peaks of the northern Cairngorms. The
circuit of Loch Morlich is very popular,
with lots of good places to stop and enjoy
the views.

This route starts from the large car park
at the far end of the loch on the Ski Road
from Coylumbridge and Aviemore, signed
'Loch Morlich Watersports'. The Aviemore
bus calls here. Any of the other car parks

alongside Loch Morlich would also make
suitable start points for this walk. The
circuit of the loch is marked almost all the
way by dark red marker posts.

Begin opposite the entrance to the car
park and head past the wooden toilet block.
(The large beach a short way to the right is
well worth the diversion.) As the red marker
posts lead you clockwise round the loch,
you cross a small wooden footbridge and
pass Loch Morlich Campsite on your left.

Further on, the trail reaches the fast-
flowing Abhain Ruigh-eunachan, close to
where it empties into Loch Morlich. Turn
left upstream to reach a bridge. Cross this,
turning right on the far side: for a short
while the route follows white markers
which guide you left away from the burn
on a meandering course. According to

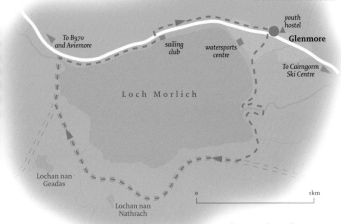

legend, these forests are haunted by the Lamh Dheag ('the Bloody Hand' in Gaelic), a giant spectre who gives battle to wanderers lost among the trees at night – so make sure you keep a careful eye on those markers.

When you come to a junction with a wider path, turn right, keeping right again at a fork to return to the shore of the loch. There are fabulous views across the water to the Monadhliath and, further on, Meall a'Bhuachaille, the small mountain which sits directly above the visitor centre and is perfectly mirrored in the still surface of the loch on a calm day.

The walk continues around the far side of the loch, passing plenty of points where you can access the shore. Simply keep to the clear track, veering right at a junction and noting the red marker posts once more. After a while, the route crosses a small ford, with a wooden bridge enabling walkers to keep feet dry.

Carry on until you reach a wide T-junction, where you turn right to meet a green metal bridge and the main road from Aviemore. Immediately after the bridge, take the path on the right which hugs the shores of the loch. You'll pass a number of sandy beaches here which make for tempting stops, though they are close to the road. Shortly before the sailing club building is a large sandy area where you can enjoy the classic view across the water to Cairn Gorm and Braeriach – the perfect setting for a picnic.

At the end of the beach, but before the clubhouse, cross the road and follow the signs for walkers and cyclists onto the path which runs parallel to it. This leads all the way to the Forestry Commission visitor centre (shop, café, toilets) at Glenmore. To return to the start, turn right down a steep path opposite the car park entrance and cross the road.

Craigellachie Woods over Aviemore

Distance 2.5km **Time** 1 hour
Terrain rocky, waymarked paths
Map OS Explorer OL57 **Access** Aviemore is
well served by buses and trains

The Craigellachie National Nature
Reserve provides a quick escape from the
bustle of Aviemore, just a few minutes'
walk away. With the chance to spot rare
plants and perhaps even peregrine
falcons, this woodland reserve is a
popular site with great views back over
Aviemore to the grand wall of the
Cairngorms range.

Car parking for the reserve is shared
with the SYHA hostel which can be found
at the southern end of Aviemore,
signposted off the main road on the left
as you enter town. Inside the hostel there
is a free information display and a

peregrine CCTV nestcam with live
streaming during the nesting season.
There are also toilets and a café.

Follow the signed path to the right of
the car park to soon go down through a
tunnel under the thunderingly busy A9.
This point can also be joined from the
rear of the Aviemore Highland Resort by
a link path which passes to the right of
the play area and pond.

Once under the A9, the path
immediately plunges into the birch
woodland that covers the reserve from the
road almost to the top of the high cliffs
behind. Birches thrive in poor but well-
drained soils, and Craigellachie is thought
to have been continually wooded for at
least 150 years. The name comes from the
Gaelic *Creag Eileachaidh*, meaning 'the Crag
of the Rocky Place' – and it is easy to see

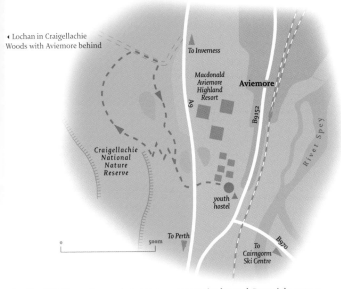

◀ Lochan in Craigellachie
Woods with Aviemore behind

To Inverness

Macdonald
Aviemore
Highland
Resort

Aviemore

A9

B9152

River Spey

Craigellachie
National
Nature
Reserve

youth
hostel

0   500m

To Perth

To
Cairngorm
Ski Centre

B970

why. The cliffs themselves are home to a nesting pair of peregrine falcons: even if you don't spot them, you may hear their loud alarm calls. Buzzards are also frequently seen on the thermals high above. In spring, the woods are filled with wildflowers.

Follow the path which heads uphill, ignoring a branch-off to the lochan on the right. The route, marked with green arrows, rises left up the wooded slopes. As the gradient eases, a second lovely lochan comes into view below. Keep to the path as it curves around the natural rocky bowl, giving great views over the 'skyscraper' hotels of Aviemore to the

mountains beyond. Drop right onto a downhill track and, as you near the bottom, turn right again onto a path which skirts around the second lochan you could see from above, following the green arrows. During the summer months, this is a great spot for watching dragonflies and damselflies darting over the water.

Cross a small burn and continue on the meandering path, taking a right-hand turn at a fork and then right again. Beyond this, you rejoin the outward path: keep left here and retrace your steps through the tunnel and back towards the car park by the hostel.

29

Loch an Eilein and Loch Gamhna

Distance 7km **Time** 2 hours
Terrain good paths and tracks; can be
muddy around Loch Gamhna
Map OS Explorer OL57 **Access** bus from
Aviemore to Inverdruie, 2km by various
trails from start (visit Rothiemurchus
Visitor Centre for maps and information)

**This popular circuit around Loch an Eilein
explores one of the most enchanting
parts of the ancient Rothiemurchus pine
forest, with a detour to its quieter and
wilder neighbour – Loch Gamhna.**

The walk begins from the Loch an Eilein
car park (fee) at the end of the minor road
to the loch. By the entrance, the estate has
put up bird feeders which attract many
small birds, including crested tits –
characteristic of the pinewoods – but you
may also see inquisitive red squirrels
which frequently carry out daring
raids on the peanuts.

At the far end of the car park,
take the path signposted for Loch
an Eilein. You'll shortly see a small
white cottage on the right. This was
once home to the estate's stonemason

but is now an information centre. Inside,
you can find out more about the area,
including the history of timber production
dating back to the early 18th century, and
the wildlife that lives here today. There is a
display aimed at children, allowing them
to touch items from the forest.

From the information centre, return to
the path and turn left to begin the
clockwise circuit of the loch. Cross the
outflow from the loch on a small
footbridge before climbing up a little way
through the fine pinewoods.

Pass a white cottage and go through a
gate. Continue on the main path, ignoring
a branch to the left, and cross a second
bridge. At the next fork, keep right; the left

Map labels:
To B970 and Aviemore
information centre
Loch an Eilein Cottage
ruin
Loch an Eilein
To Lairig Ghru
Inshriach
Loch Gamhna
0   1km

branch leads to the Lairig Ghru, the high mountain pass that today makes a popular, though epic, trek through the Cairngorms to emerge near Braemar on Deeside.

The path soon returns to the loch shore, giving great views across the water. Loch an Eilein is a feeding spot for ospreys that nest nearby so, between April and August, there is a good chance of seeing one of these magnificent birds on a fishing trip. Most of the Rothiemurchus pinewoods are very mature, with many parts dating back to the ancient Caledonian forest itself, but now the route passes through a clearer area which young, scattered trees are beginning to recolonise. At an easily-missed junction, next to some fire beaters, turn left off the main path to include the rougher round of Loch Gamhna. Some parts of this path can be muddy, and it can be missed out by simply continuing ahead and over the footbridge. Otherwise, for Loch Gamhna, keep right at an unmarked fork and follow the path as it slopes down and then skirts around the edge of this very attractive smaller loch. Once around

the sometimes boggy head of the loch, the path tackles the far shores and passes a number of 'granny' pines – so called because of their great age. Rejoin the main Loch an Eilein circular at a T-junction and turn left. At the next junction (footpath sign), turn right for the final stretch along the north shore, passing through a gate and in front of Loch an Eilein Cottage in its idyllic situation. Just offshore is the island that gives the loch its name, crowned with a ruined 14th-century castle. In the 1800s, the ruins were the site of an osprey eyrie before the birds were driven away by egg collectors, part of the persecution that led to their extinction from Britain. Although the ospreys returned to nearby Loch Garten in 1954, they have never again nested on the castle. Continue on the main track to return to the start.

To the Ryvoan Pass

Distance 10.5km **Time** 3 hours
Terrain waymarked paths and tracks;
short, steep section **Map** OS Explorer
OL57 **Access** bus from Aviemore and
Grantown-on-Spey. Car park (charge)
at Glenmore

A beautiful walk which takes in a great
variety of scenery, heading up through
the remains of the ancient Glenmore
pinewoods to reach the startling
turquoise waters of An Lochan Uaine.
From there, you can journey to a lonely
bothy through the steep-sided glacial
trench of the Ryvoan Pass with a riverside
return to the sands of Loch Morlich.

The route begins from the Glenmore
Visitor Centre. Head up to the visitor
centre building, skirting around it on the
left to reach a track. A path with a blue and
orange marker post climbs steeply uphill
opposite. This leads you through forestry
to a track, where you turn right: the blue

waymarkers continue for the whole walk.
Just before it comes to a house, the route
joins another track and turns left on a
gentle rise past the old, twisted and
characterful Scots pines known as
'grannies'. The track ends beyond a seat
with views over to Cairn Gorm.

Ahead, a rougher pathway takes its
place, levelling off for a while before
heading downhill on a series of
boardwalks at first and then a rough flight
of steps, passing some lovely scattered
pines on the way. At the bottom, you join
a path coming in from the right and turn
left to reach An Lochan Uaine. A tiny
detour down to the loch edge reveals the
translucent blue-green hue of the water
even on a dull day. Legend has it that this
colouring was caused by fairies washing
their clothes in it: no mention is made as
to whether they were using a certain brand
of washing up liquid.

The main track climbs uphill to the left,

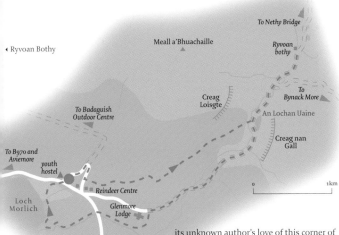

To Nethy Bridge

Meall a'Bhuachaille

◄ Ryvoan Bothy

Ryvoan bothy

Creag Loisgte

To Bynack More

An Lochan Uaine

To Badaguish Outdoor Centre

Creag nan Gall

To B970 and Aviemore

youth hostel

Reindeer Centre

Loch Morlich

Glenmore Lodge

0   1km

To Cairngorm Ski Centre

its unknown author's love of this corner of the hills. After a break at the bothy, turn back downhill and retrace your steps to An Lochan Uaine, then continue on the main track down the glen for almost 2km.

Just before reaching the National Outdoor Training Centre at Glenmore Lodge, turn left onto a path – again marked with a blue post. This skirts round the woods on the south side of the lodge, turning sharp left near the entrance to a rifle range used for biathlon training.

When the path reaches the river, turn right downstream. Cross straight over the Cairngorm Ski Road and accompany the river, passing but not crossing a bridge.

The trail swings to the right just short of Loch Morlich and runs through the pinewoods set back from the fine beach. Turn right beside the wooden public toilets to follow the route across the edge of the campsite and back to the start.

soon crossing more open moorland at the pass itself. At an obvious fork, take the left-hand branch, signed for Nethy Bridge. The right-hand route is the start of the Lairig an Laoigh, a high and challenging pass once busy with cattle drovers, which leads eventually to the Linn of Dee and Braemar. Just beyond the top of a rise on the left-hand path you will find Ryvoan Bothy, an old stone cottage providing an open shelter to walkers. It is maintained by volunteers from the Mountain Bothies Association who have to carry heavy materials up to this beautiful spot for repairs: please help them by carrying out any litter you find here. A poem was written on the back of the door at Ryvoan during the Second World War, celebrating

Corrie of the Snows

Distance 6km **Time** 3 hours **Terrain** well-made path, exposed to the elements **Map** OS Explorer OL57 **Access** bus from Aviemore and Grantown-on-Spey

An escape from the busy developments of the Cairngorm Ski Centre to enter a high mountain corrie popular with ice and rock climbers. The path is good and in fair weather the walk is straightforward. However, at this altitude conditions can deteriorate rapidly and full hillwalking clothing plus map and compass are necessary. When the path is under snow, it should be left to the experts.

Start the walk from the Coire Cas car park. This is the base for the Cairngorm Funicular Railway and Ski Centre, which stands at 620m above sea level – an extremely exposed place in bad weather. The footpath begins at the top right-hand end of the car park, heading away from the buildings. There are steps up to this point

from the lower level of the car park. Cross a small bridge and climb a few steps to the right of the lowest ski tow. Looking down, there are fabulous views out over the great green carpet of Rothiemurchus Forest and Loch Morlich to Aviemore, with the rounded bulk of the Monadhliath beyond.

A well-made path leads you, after a short distance, to a fork, where you should take the higher path on the left. The lower path passes Coire an Lochain before climbing up towards the summits. A *coire* is a steep-sided bowl or corrie, scooped from the mountainside by glaciers during the last ice age. The Cairngorms have scores of spectacular examples, those on this side of Cairn Gorm being collectively known as the Northern Corries. They contain some of Britain's most impressive and popular mountaineering routes.

As you gain height, keep to the main path and ignore a fainter one which forks off to the right later on. After a while, the

◄ Looking down to Loch Morlich from the path to Coire an t-Sneachda

path starts to climb more steeply and crosses the burn before shadowing it towards the cliffs of Coire an t-Sneachda ahead. The path loses definition as it wanders amongst the stones and finally ends just before an area of huge boulders in the floor of the corrie. You can either stop here or cross the boulders with care to reach the tiny lochans below the cliffs.

Coire an t-Sneachda means 'the Corrie of the Snows' in Gaelic. In the summer months, you may spot climbers edging up the great buttresses on rock routes with evocative names such as Pygmy Ridge or the Magic Crack, but it is for winter climbing that Coire an t-Sneachda is renowned. North-facing and shaded from the sun, it retains snow and ice late in the year. When conditions are right, ice climbers can be seen roped together in the cold and shadowy gullies, swinging their axes above their heads and kicking in their crampon points. Visiting the corrie when there is snow on the path requires winter hillwalking gear and experience – you

should check weather conditions before you go and take the relevant OS map and a compass – but the reward is a likely sighting of climbers making their way up these ice-clad precipices. Retrace your steps to the ski centre, where you'll find a shop and cosy bar in the Day Lodge at the foot of the mountain or take the railway to the Ptarmigan Restaurant at the top.

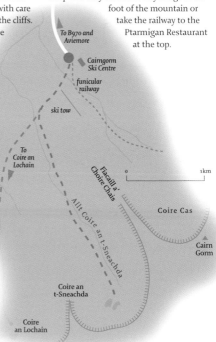

Rothiemurchus and the Iron Bridge

Distance 7km **Time** 2 hours
Terrain very good paths, mostly level
Map OS Explorer OL57 **Access** bus from
Aviemore and Grantown-on-Spey

This almost level circuit explores one of
the finest areas of Caledonian pinewood
to be found in the Rothiemurchus Estate,
giving amazing mountain views without
a climb. There is an excellent chance of
spotting red squirrels and other wildlife,
whilst the riverside near the Iron Bridge
makes for a lovely, remote picnic site.

The walk starts along the lane next to
Rothiemurchus Camp and Caravan Park at
Coylumbridge. If driving there is parking
in a lay-by just off the main road in
Coylumbridge. Follow the lane past the

campsite and the now derelict Lairig Ghru
Cottage, then pass through the gate into
the forest. Where the track forks, take the
left-hand path signed for the Lairig Ghru:
this shadows the river for a short while
before heading through some of the
beautiful mature pinewoods for which the
Rothiemurchus Estate is famous.

After crossing a small bridge and then a
gateside stile, continue straight ahead,
passing through another gate in a stone
wall where the track soon narrows. Cross a
second bridge and carry on along the
narrowing path to shortly come to the
edge of some dense plantation forestry.
The Cairngorm mountains can be seen
ahead, with the deep scree-flanked pass of
the Lairig Ghru at the centre. The Lairig

Ghru is a high foot pass, traditionally used as a major route across the mountains from Deeside to Strathspey. Today, it is popular as a challenge for strong walkers, with the full route from Aviemore to Braemar stretching for 43km and rising to 835m – though many people finish at the Linn of Dee, 8km short of Braemar. An annual race completes it in its entirety: the record time is an amazing three hours and four minutes.

At an obvious junction, carry straight on to soon reach the Iron Bridge, which makes a pretty rest stop. Also known as the Cairngorm Club Footbridge after the climbers' club which built it in 1912, its construction across the fast-flowing Am Beanaidh made the full Lairig Ghru accessible once more. After admiring the river from the bridge, backtrack as far as the last fork. This time, take the left-hand option signed for Loch an Eilein, passing through an area of regenerating forest.

Look out for the attractive Lochan Deo on your left, where in summer you're likely to spy many dragonflies. After diving into dense forestry, you come to a crossroads. Turn right here for a spell on a gently rising track, emerging through a wooden gate into more open countryside. There are superb views back to Cairn Gorm and its ski slopes, with the Lairig Ghru appearing as a great cleft further right. The path continues straight on, crossing a grassy area scattered with some ancient granny pines, relics from the massive Caledonian forest that once covered most of Scotland. Disregard the smaller track heading left uphill, and continue until you eventually reach a metal gate and cattle grid: beyond the stile, go straight on through the trees to return to the start.

‹ Lochan Deo with Braeriach in the background

37

Meall a'Bhuachaille from Glenmore

Distance 8km **Time** 4 hours 30
Terrain good paths; a climb to a high
summit, very exposed in bad weather
Map OS Explorer OL57 **Access** bus from
Aviemore and Grantown-on-Spey

The most strenuous walk in this book,
the ascent of Meall a'Bhuachaille is well
worth the effort, revealing magnificent
views over Loch Morlich, Strathspey and
the Cairngorms. The path is good, but
hillwalking clothes, a map and compass
are needed in case the weather closes in.

Meall a'Bhuachaille's Gaelic name
means 'Rounded Hill of the Herdsman':
its slopes were once used for grazing by
the many surrounding farms, keen to take
advantage of some of the most fertile soil
in the Cairngorms.

There are several routes of ascent, the

shortest being the well-made path from
Glenmore Visitor Centre. Begin by skirting
round the left side of the building, going
straight across a track onto a path
opposite, where you immediately make a
steep uphill climb. The route of ascent has
orange waymarkers as far as the treeline,
but is unmarked higher up. At a T-junction,
turn left for a more gentle climb through
dense forestry plantations. Glenmore was
purchased by the Forestry Commission
after the First World War when shortages
made the production of fast-growing
timber a priority. Today, efforts are
underway to expand the native pinewoods
and improve the biodiversity of the habitat.

The route runs alongside a small burn,
ignoring the path that crosses the water at
a junction to instead remain on the east
bank. After a felled area, the plantations

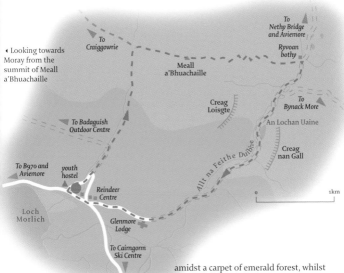

‹ Looking towards Moray from the summit of Meall a'Bhuachaille

give way to natural forest with some magnificently-twisted old pines. These scattered relics are now joined by many younger trees as natural generation takes hold. As it gains altitude, the path leaves the last trees behind and reaches the ridge just above the bealach (or saddle-shaped pass) between Meall a'Bhuachaille and neighbouring Creagan Gorm. Turn right here for the final toil up to the summit, marked by a cairn and windshelter.

Meall a'Bhuachaille is 810m high and its position, detached from the main Cairngorms range, gives superb views in all directions, with Loch Morlich glinting amidst a carpet of emerald forest, whilst Cairn Gorm and its neighbours rise to their full stature. To the northeast, the huge RSPB reserve of Abernethy Forest makes a fine foreground to the range upon range of lower hills leading the eye away into Moray and the sea beyond.

The quickest return is to retrace your steps, but the longer return follows the recently reconstructed path down the eastern flanks of the hill to the lonely bothy at Ryvoan. Here, you turn right down the track, carrying straight on at a junction to head through the Ryvoan Pass and meet the public road end at Glenmore Lodge. From here, a new path on the right-hand side of the road leads back to Glenmore Visitor Centre.

Nethy Bridge and Dell Woods

Distance 3km **Time** 1 hour
Terrain good paths, tracks, minor road
Map OS Explorer OL57 **Access** buses from
Aviemore and Grantown-on-Spey

**A very pleasant short circular, first along
the banks of the River Nethy and then
through the lovely Dell Woods National
Nature Reserve, returning to the village of
Nethy Bridge. This easy family walk offers
plenty of variety.**

Start from Nethy Bridge Community
Centre, on the south side of the river,
where you'll find parking and toilets – as
well as an exhibition (open in summer
only) detailing the fascinating history of
Abernethy Forest and the surrounding
area, with hands-on activities for children.
There is often a ranger on duty who can
advise on local walks, including the
waymarked trails around the village.

This route begins along the wooded
riverside path opposite the community
centre. Historically, timber has played a
massive part in the local economy and, as
you follow the river upstream, it is
possible to imagine felled trees being
transported downstream to join the great
River Spey where they were then floated
all the way to the sea at Spey Bay on the
Moray Firth. The water level would have
been no different to that today, but a
series of dams and sluices upstream
enabled it to be stored, sending hundreds
of tree trunks down the crashing waters
when released. This practice continued
until the arrival of the steam railway here.

After meandering along the riverbank,
the path emerges on a minor road by a
house. Turn left here and carry on along
the road to pass, but not cross, an
attractive green footbridge. The road turns

◄ Footbridge over the River Nethy at Lower Dell

sharp right and passes some pretty cottages. Go directly across a T-junction to follow a ruler-straight path, flanked on both sides by beech hedging. To keep a constant supply of timber, the felled areas of the forest were constantly replanted. The beech hedges and two large Wellingtonia (giant redwoods) on either side of the path mark the entrance to what was once a nursery, established in 1855 to raise pine seedlings for the restocking of the forest. Now, natural regeneration techniques are preferred and the nursery was closed in 1984. Continue straight ahead at a small crossroads, following the blue and green arrows as the narrowing path wends its way into a lovely area of coniferous woodland dominated by Scots pine. This is Dell Woods, much loved by residents of Nethy Bridge and now a National Nature Reserve: it sits on the edge of the village.

Where the path approaches the corner of a large white house, turn left to carry on through the forest by the arrowed signs. The path runs behind several houses before bearing left and diving deeper into the trees. When you meet a larger track, follow the green arrow sign straight ahead to dip downhill. Just beyond a grazing field on the right, the track emerges from the wood onto a road. Turn right here, walking past the houses towards the centre of Nethy Bridge. Just before the river, turn left to return to the community centre and the start of the walk.

To
Grantown
-on-Spey

B970

To
Aviemore

Nethy Bridge

shop

football
pitch

River Nethy

Dell Road

To
Lettoch

0   500m

Castle Roy and Craigmore Wood

Distance 5.5km **Time** 1 hour 30
Terrain waymarked forest paths
Map OS Explorer OL57 **Access** buses from
Aviemore and Grantown-on-Spey

This figure-of-eight walk loops through
the forests to the north of Nethy
Bridge, passing the ruins of Castle Roy, a fortress
dating back to the 13th century.

Start from the Balnagowan Wood car
park. To reach it from the centre of Nethy
Bridge, follow the road through the north
side of the village and turn left in the
settlement of Causar. The car park is on
the left, whilst the walk begins on the
opposite side of the road. A path with pink
marker posts leads you through the trees
behind a row of back gardens. Keep
straight ahead after the gardens, crossing a
small bridge and steering left when a
larger path joins in from the village. The
path comes close to a minor road before

running through the woods parallel to it.
Go through an informal turning area and
keep straight on before branching left at
a marker post to head deeper into the
trees. After passing a small lochan, turn
right for an uphill climb, eventually
reaching a stile and crossing a minor road
onto a track beyond.

When you come to a T-junction, turn
right following the sign for Castle Roy. The
pink arrows indicate a left turn onto a path
which runs alongside an obstacle course
and over a footbridge. The route becomes
more open as it swings left and climbs to a
white cottage. Turn left through a gate,
passing directly left of the cottage where
the drive leads you to a church by a road.

A right turn onto the road brings you to
the ruins of Castle Roy in the field on your
left. The simple stone keep has a strategic
position overlooking the Spey Valley, with
massive walls that are still more than 2m

thick and 7m tall at their highest. It is thought that wooden structures once divided the large interior which was probably covered by a roof, though no signs of these have been found. The castle was intended as a refuge to hide people, animals and valuables from raiders, although much of its history remains a mystery.

Beyond the castle, a gate gives access to a path which runs parallel to the road. Turn right onto a track to wind back through the woods, ignoring a turn-off to the left (which heads to Grantown) further on. After 1km, look for a red arrow indicating a small path on the right; this passes close to some white cottages with glimpses of the grand house of Aultmore as it descends. Aultmore was built in the early 1900s by the owner of a Moscow department store.

The path turns left just before a farm gate, and then bears right between a wall and a fence. It skirts above a bank before emerging by the white cottage that you passed on the way to Castle Roy. Turn left, retracing your outward route over the bridge, and veering right onto the track.

When you reach the T-junction by a chalet, the most straightforward route is to carry straight on, following the sign for the

village (no pink marker this time). At the road, go straight ahead until you rejoin the pink markers which indicate a left turn into the woods. The path runs close to the fence of Abernethy Primary School, turning right at a corner. Cross a tiny bridge and go through a kissing gate. The path from here has been improved for children on their walk to school; follow the path which runs parallel to the road back to Nethy Bridge. Just before the houses, go right and cross the road to the Balnagowan Wood car park at the start.

◀ Castle Roy

Loch Garten osprey loop

Distance 9km **Time** 2 hours 30
Terrain fairly level woodland paths; brief
muddy sections **Map** OS Explorer OL57
Access bus from Aviemore and
Grantown-on-Spey to Boat of Garten
(or take the Strathspey Steam Railway
from Aviemore in summer), 1km from
start via the Speyside Way

This walk visits Loch Garten, famous for
its osprey eyrie, and the more secretive
Loch Mallachie. An optional detour to the
RSPB visitor centre offers the chance to
view live CCTV footage of the ospreys in
summer and join a variety of nature-
based ranger activities.

Start from the Garten Woods car park on
the B970, opposite the junction with the
Boat of Garten road. An information board
gives details of shorter waymarked trails
in the area. Pass the board and bear right,
keeping to the red trail markers at first as
you follow a wandering course through
the woods. At a fork, stay right for a
stretch of forest path which delves deeper
into the trees. Although most of it is Scots
pine, this section of the wood was
originally a plantation. Now part of the
RSPB's vast Abernethy Forest Estate, work
has been carried out to restore the habitat
to a more natural state, with vehicle tracks
removed and trees thinned out. The boggy
forest floor either side of the path makes
an excellent habitat for a number of
species, and the RSPB is deliberately
keeping the water table high here. On
some of the drier sections, you may spot
large mounds of pine needles: these are
wood ant nests, an important member of a
food chain that supports such prized
species such as the Scottish crossbill and
the crested tit.

Keep an eye out for a narrow path on the
left after about 1km. (If you reach a sharp
right turn with a path leading on ahead, you
have gone too far and need to backtrack for
100m.) Stick to this main path as it
undulates through the trees before arriving

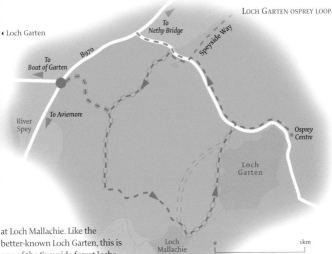

◄ Loch Garten

To Nethy Bridge

B970

To Boat of Garten

To Aviemore

River Spey

Speyside Way

Osprey Centre

Loch Garten

Loch Mallachie

0   1km

at Loch Mallachie. Like the better-known Loch Garten, this is one of the Speyside forest lochs which have become a habitat for ospreys in summer and an overwintering destination for geese, goldeneye ducks and swans. With no public access for cars, the serene beauty of Loch Mallachie is little disturbed by human activity, the water fringed by pines on three sides with a view to the mountains beyond.

At a waymarked T-junction, turn right where, soon afterwards, the path bears sharp left away from the loch and edges towards the larger Loch Garten. Several short detour paths to the water's edge fan off on the right. Continue ahead at a fork to reach a small car park. From here, follow the trail up to the tarmac road, crossing it and climbing the bank to reach a path running parallel with the road on the far side. Turn left to continue the walk or right for a detour to the Osprey Centre.

Loch Garten was where ospreys first built their eyrie when they returned to Scotland in the 1960s. These amazing fish-eating birds spend the winter in Africa, arriving back in Scotland in late March before leaving again in August or September. During this time, live CCTV footage from the nest is shown in the centre.

Back on the route, you soon join a section of the long-distance Speyside Way, which follows the course of the Spey past fine distilleries to the sea. Turn left and cross the road here, bearing right on the far side: a path leads to a small forest lochan where a wooden walkway gives a closer view of the thriving dragon and damselflies. The path shortly meets a wider one, which plunges left into the forest. This eventually rejoins the outward route and returns to the car park.

Ellan Wood from Carrbridge

Distance 3.5km **Time** 1 hour
Terrain easy and fairly level woodland
paths **Map** OS Explorer OL60
Access Carrbridge is served by buses and
trains (station 1km from centre)

On the very edge of the popular village
of Carrbridge is Ellan Wood. This fine
pinewood is the setting for several short,
waymarked walks which together make
this slightly longer outing.

Carrbridge is famous for its distinctive
humpbacked packhorse bridge which
dates back to 1717. Its strange appearance
as a thin but graceful single arch is
a reminder of the 'Muckle Spate' of 1829 –
a great flood, said to be the worst ever
experienced in Britain, which ripped the
parapets from the sides. To reach the start
of the route, leave the main street to go
down Station Road by the bridge, then
take the left turn, signed for Ellan Wood,

where there is a picnic area and parking
next to a cemetery.

An information board gives details of
the various short walks here: this route
initially follows the yellow markers. Begin
on the path to the left of the sign, keeping
left at the first junction, then straight on
when a short loop of path heads to the
right. Keep left at the next junction where
there is a bench (SP Main Street). When a
path comes in from Carrbridge on the left
turn right (SP Boat of Garten via Carr
Plantation Trail) to head further into the
woods, following the red waymarkers.

Carry straight on at a crossroads and
again at a three-way fork to follow the red
waymarkers (SP Railway Wood walk).
Cross an access track and soon after pass a
striking wooden tower – the highest in
Britain and part of the Landmark Forest
Adventure Park. Continue through the
dense plantation of Scots pines, eventually

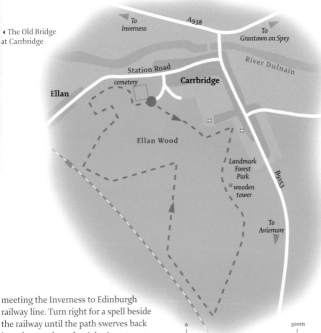

◄ The Old Bridge
at Carrbridge

meeting the Inverness to Edinburgh
railway line. Turn right for a spell beside
the railway until the path swerves back
into the woods to the right. In autumn,
the woodland floor reveals an astonishing
array of fungi – both in terms of size and
variety – and there is a good chance of
spotting a red squirrel high in the trees.

At a T-junction, turn left. This part of
Ellan Wood is owned by the Woodland
Trust and has a much more natural feel.
There are lichen-encrusted birches and
great, gnarled old pines with real
character. You are now following the
yellow markers again; bear sharp right

down a flight of wooden steps at one
point, later crossing two small wooden
bridges. The next intersection has two
wonderfully carved, high-backed wooden
benches: take a left here through a
particularly beautiful section of pinewood,
keeping right at two further junctions.
When the cemetery comes into view
ahead, skirt around the edge to the right
to return to the start.

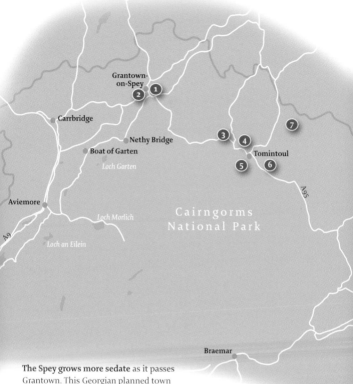

The Spey grows more sedate as it passes Grantown. This Georgian planned town has an airy, tree-lined square – as well as many historic buildings, independent shops and cafés popular with visitors. The setting is stately too, with Anagach Woods taking up much of the valley floor on one side of town whilst gentle hills rise up from the other.

Just over the rolling Cromdale Hills is Tomintoul, its 354m above the sea giving rise to its claim to be the highest village in the Highlands. Built by the Duke of

Gordon in 1775, partly in an effort to stamp out illegal distilling in the area, its exposed location makes it a cold and windy place, often snowbound in winter.

From here, the River Avon and its tributary, the Livet, carve their winding courses down through the bare and lonely hills to the Spey. The names Glenlivet and Speyside need no introduction to connoisseurs of a dram – this is the heart of malt whisky country.

48 Red squirrel ▶

Grantown-on-Spey and Tomintoul

Anagach Woods and the Speyside Way

Distance 11.5km **Time** 3 hours
Terrain woodland and riverside paths
Map OS Explorer OL61 **Access** Grantown-on-Spey is well served by buses

On the fringes of Grantown-on-Spey, this community-owned woodland is home to three generations of Scots pine and remains one of the last refuges of the capercaillie: it is important that walkers keep dogs under close control and stick to main paths. This walk also takes in a beautiful section of the Spey riverbank and the lovely settlement of Speybridge.

From the centre of Grantown, walk up the High Street to the wide section known as The Square. On the east side, opposite the Co-op, turn into Forest Road – which is signposted for the Speyside Way, River Spey and Anagach Woods. Carry straight on at the staggered crossroads. The road runs alongside the golf course before coming to a parking area for the woods. Turn left by the interpretative panels: the route is signed for 'Speyside Way to Cromdale' for the first stretch. Ignore a green-waymarked turn-off to the right and instead keep ahead, following the Speyside Way thistle symbols.

At the next junction, go left through the gate. The track soon reaches a clearing where the route may not be apparent: keep left and eventually you'll come to the next Speyside Way marker. The trail plunges back into the pines before coming close to the edge, where there is a view across to the golf clubhouse. Here the path widens as it bears right, penetrating deeper into Anagach Woods. The woodland was originally planted in 1766 with trees from nearby Abernethy Forest, but began to regenerate naturally by the early 19th century and the trees seen today are almost entirely self-seeded. The deeper parts of the woods are one of the last refuges of the remarkable capercaillie, a giant black grouse as big as a turkey, whose name means 'The Horse of the Woods' in Gaelic, referring to the clip-clop sound it makes.

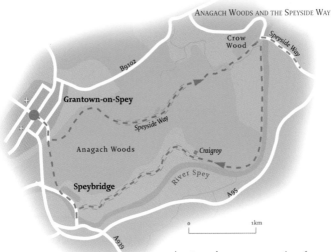

Stick to the main path, steering slightly left at a junction and continuing to follow the thistle marker posts. The route undulates over ancient glacial ridges as it winds between some magnificent old trees. Keep left at the next junction and left again at a fork to eventually reach a gate and then a bridge. After crossing this, head right along the edge of Crow Wood to reach the River Spey.

Ahead, there's an old iron bridge carrying a minor road over the Spey, but this route turns sharp right before the bridge, going through a gate to follow a riverbank trail upstream. At the edge of Craigroy Wood, there is a fishing lodge. The Spey is one of Scotland's big four salmon rivers and has given its name to a method of casting. Anglers clad in thigh-high waders can often be seen standing almost motionless far out in the current. Continue through dense

pines to reach a more open section of riverbank. After a short climb away from the river, you reach the lonely house at Craigroy, where you join a track and pass through a gate, keeping straight on at a junction. Beyond Mid Anagach and the splendid old Anagach Lodge, carry straight on, passing a second more modern lodge before the road slopes down to Speybridge.

It is worth detouring left here to see the striking old bridge over the Spey that gives this hamlet its name. Return to Grantown by following the road past the beautiful houses of Speybridge and turning right back into the woods at the Speyside Way sign. The route now follows the Old Military Road, which runs arrow-straight between the pines. Ignore all turnings on both sides, eventually passing through a gate to reach the Anagach Woods car park. Carry on ahead, back past the fire station to the centre of Grantown.

◄ River Spey near Speybridge

Viewpoints Walk from Grantown

Distance 5km Time 1 hour 30
Terrain **waymarked grassy paths, some
fairly steep climbing** Map OS Explorer
OL61 Access **Grantown-on-Spey is well
served by buses**

**Look out over Grantown-on-Spey from
the lower slopes of Gorton Hill. This
waymarked route climbs up to a pine-
clad, rocky crag with a viewpoint marker
showing the distant Cairngorms
summits, before descending back to the
town via the old railway line.**

Grantown has a bustling main street
that widens at the north end with lawns
on either side and a grand old courthouse.
The walk starts here on The Square, just to
the left of the Co-op, where you should
follow signs for the Viewpoints Walk
down Seafield Avenue, passing houses

and the caravan park at the end to go
under the old railway line.

Emerge from the railway underpass and
turn right to cross a small wooden bridge
and go through a gate. For a good view of
the waterfall, you can climb the steps to
the left, but return to the gate to take the
right-hand fork. This leads up onto the old
railway, now part of the Dava Way, a new
37km route connecting Grantown to
Forres and passing historic Dallas Dhu
Distillery on the way.

Accompany the railway line left for a
short distance until a signed path directs
you off to the left, rising through open
woodland and between two wire fences to
gain rapid height. It is worth making a
short, signed detour over a stile on the left
to visit the first viewpoint, overlooking
Grantown from a bench. Return to the

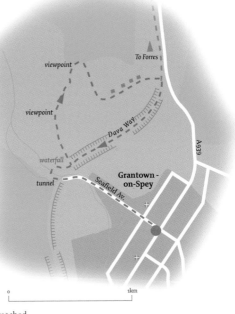

◄ Scots pine at the viewpoint above Grantown-on-Spey

main path and carry on uphill, going through two sets of gates and passing a second bench with a great view down over Speyside.

The path narrows as it weaves through mixed woodland which includes a number of large juniper bushes. At a fence and an open field, it heads up towards the right and continues through the trees before joining a track for a little while. Soon the highest of the viewpoints is reached, crowned by a group of gnarled old Scots pines and an indicator to help identify the distant Cairngorms summits.

Follow the marker post at the far end of the pines, passing a twisted tree to descend to a clearer path below the crag. Keeping to the right of a fence, the path continues straight on to join a track which goes through a farm gate and then passes a number of houses on the left before coming to the old railway line at a missing bridge. Turn right along the old railway line (left takes you along the Dava Way to Forres), heading through a deep railway cutting where green moss and ferns create a dank, tropical feel. Pass above the caravan park to return to the junction on the right, where you can descend from the line to rejoin the outward part of the route. After going through the gate and under the railway bridge, follow the road back into the centre of Grantown-on-Spey.

Glen Brown round

Distance 7km **Time** 3 hours
Terrain waymarked paths and tracks,
undulating ground with roadside
return **Map** OS Explorer OL58
Access no public transport

This varied circumnavigation of the small
hill of Tom Beag gives ever-changing
views over the bare slopes of Glen Avon
and Glen Brown.

The walk begins from the White Bridge
car park, situated on a bend at the top of
the steep rise on the A939 to Tomintoul,
not far from the Bridge of Brown. This is
one of a number of routes waymarked by
the Glenlivet Estate, and appears on signs
as 'No. 8'. The track skirts along the right-
hand side of the Tom an Marbh plantation,
following the line of an old military road
built by the prolific Major Caulfeild
(successor to the more famous General

Wade), which ran for more than 160km
from Blairgowrie in Perthshire to Fort
George on the Moray Firth. After about
350m, the track reaches the crest of the hill
and begins to drop downhill, passing
through a gate and swinging to the right to
avoid entering the forest.

After a zigzag descent towards the
modern road, leave the track at a sharp left
bend and continue straight ahead up a
couple of steps and past some marker
posts. On this section, the path is faint so
keep looking out for the small wooden
markers. Beyond a bench with a fine view
over Glen Avon, descend a gentle, grassy
slope: your approach is likely to send
rabbits scattering in all directions.

The path weaves through clumps of
juniper bushes and alongside a fence at
the top of a wood. At the next fence, climb
a stile and pass below a small section of

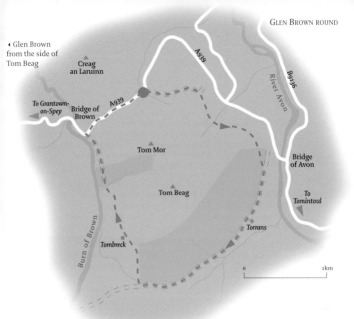

◄ Glen Brown
from the side of
Tom Beag

Creag
an Laruinn

A939

B9136

River Avon

To Grantown-
on-Spey

Bridge of
Brown

A939

Tom Mor

Bridge
of Avon

Tom Beag

To
Tomintoul

Burn of Brown

Torrans

Tombreck

0   1km

trees to reach a second stile, continuing to
drop through some attractive deciduous
woodland. The path runs beside another
fence to reach a third stile.

Turn right onto the track here and keep
right at a fork. Almost immediately, the
track forks again: this time, head left and
go through a gate into a plantation of
conifers. After 1km, the dense tree cover is
left behind at a gate: turn right through
this to head straight uphill onto grassy
moorland, with good views into the wild
upper reaches of Glen Brown.

Now the climbing eases and there is a
short drop before you tackle the hill
ahead. Once past the fence in the dip, take
a grassy track which forks off to the left.

This rises slightly and passes through a
gap, then begins to descend across the
slopes. It curves to the right and passes
the ruins of an old farmhouse. There are
several other ruined hill farms in view
here, showing how this was once a more
densely populated area.

Eventually, the track heads through
a brief section of forestry and almost
meets the A939, close to the river. Just
before you reach it, though, a waymarker
indicates a right turn that keeps you off-
road for a little longer. Unfortunately,
when it does rejoin it there is no
alternative to the steep roadside climb,
watching out for traffic as you return to
the car park and the start.

Tomintoul tour to Carn Daimh

Distance 11km **Time** 3 hours 30
Terrain steady climb on forest tracks,
descent on heathery moorland paths and
grassy pastures **Map** OS Explorer OL61
Access bus to Tomintoul, 5km from the
start via the Speyside Way

Carn Daimh offers a fine perspective over
the rolling hillcountry of Glenlivet,
between Ben Rinnes and the Cairngorms.
This waymarked ascent takes in farmland,
forest and open heather moorland.
A perfect leg stretcher before or after
visiting one of the nearby distilleries.

   This is one of several walks laid out by
the Glenlivet Estate and is 'No. 6' on the
waymarker posts. A parking area has been
provided in front of Glenconglass Cottage,
about 2.5km from Tomintoul off a minor
loop from the B9008. Cross the cattle grid

at the start and follow the track through
grazing land. Keeping below the dense
plantation, ignore two tracks branching
right. The sharp-eyed may very well spot
roe deer darting through the fields or in
and out of the trees, whilst the meadows
are full of wildflowers in early summer.

   Still beneath the conifers, bear left along
the track, ignoring another track which
climbs to the left. When the forest looms
ahead, take the waymarked turn-off to the
right, crossing a bridge over a small burn.
Soon this track begins to rise, giving good
views towards Ardgieth on the left as it
runs along the edge of the trees and
finally enters the forest. Turn left onto
another track to reach a three-way fork,
where you should take the middle option
for a gentler climb through the trees.

   Eventually, after turning right at the

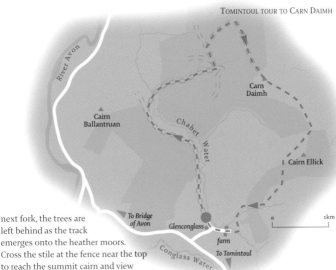

next fork, the trees are left behind as the track emerges onto the heather moors. Cross the stile at the fence near the top to reach the summit cairn and view indicator. Glenlivet looks idyllic below, with the village of Tomnavoulin and its sadly redundant distillery at its heart. Further out are some great views of the hills – from the landmark Ben Rinnes in the northeast to the Cairngorms range in the southwest.

The Speyside Way is followed for the next section. This long-distance walk runs most of the length of the River Spey from Aviemore to Buckie, with a number of offshoots and opportunities for whisky tastings at the distilleries along the way. The section on Carn Daimh forms part of a spur to Tomintoul. Begin by turning right onto the Speyside Way and following it downhill, keeping to the left of the fence to eventually reach some forestry. At the corner of the forest, enter the trees by a gate for a brief uphill climb before the track

resumes its descent. When you reach a junction, turn right, signed for Tomintoul.

Climb a stile next to a gate to return to open moorland. Keep a careful look out for a small marker post, which indicates where to turn right onto a faint path diving downhill through the heather.

Continue straight ahead, bearing right when you come to the plantation before accessing it via a stile. The path leads you down a firebreak and through a gate at the bottom into a field. Carry straight on and then, immediately after a stile, turn left, aiming for the wooden planks and bridge that will help you cross some boggy ground by the burn without getting your feet wet. Pass through a gate and the farmyard. The parking area at the start of the walk is just a short distance beyond.

◀ The forested slopes of Tom a'Chor from the Glenconglass track

Glen Avon and the Queen's View

Distance 5km **Time** 2 hours **Terrain** easy
tracks and minor road **Map** OS Explorer
OL58 **Access** bus to Tomintoul, 1km from
the start along a minor road

This circuit along a pretty section of Glen
Avon takes in a viewpoint admired by
Queen Victoria during one of her 'grand
expeditions' from Balmoral. There are
good views into the mountains, whilst the
woodland and riverside stretches give
good opportunities for wildlife spotting.

Parking can be found at the start of the
walk, almost 1km from the south end of
Tomintoul, just before Delnabo Bridge:
follow the signs for Tomintoul Country
Walk. There is a track at the end of the
parking area which, after a short while,
leads to a signed detour up steps on the
left to reach the Queen's View. Here, Queen
Victoria stopped to admire the view up

Glen Avon during one of her expeditions
from Balmoral in 1860. This seems to have
been a particularly ambitious trip,
undertaken on horseback. The Royal party
headed from Balmoral to Grantown-on-
Spey via Glen Feshie. The following day,
they returned to Balmoral via Tomintoul
and Glen Avon. The Queen does not
appear to have been overly keen on
Tomintoul, describing it as 'the most
tumbledown, poor-looking place I ever
saw'. However, she was sufficiently
impressed by the view up Glen Avon to
record it in her diary, and there is now a
viewpoint indicator giving the names of
the mountains ahead.

From the viewpoint, return to the main
track and turn left. Across the glen,
Delnabo House can be seen against a
backdrop of heather moorland. In late
summer, the moor is a mass of purple

◂ Highland cattle near Tomintoul

flowers, whilst at other times of year you'll notice striped patterns which result from the practice of controlled heather burning, providing new shoots for grouse to feed on. Keep to the higher track as it passes above a house at Keppoch, and continue along the side of the glen, crossing a bridge over a small burn.

Pass through a sparse birchwood before dropping down to traverse a field and reach the river. After crossing the iron bridge, carry straight on, then turn right onto a track to pass between a house and barn. The track rises slightly and passes another house on the right before joining the end of the public road. Cross the cattle grid and follow the road through pleasant farmland, where shaggy-coated Highland cattle can often be seen grazing.

Soon the road passes Delnabo House, turning sharp right as it draws alongside the Water of Ailnack and its confluence with the Avon. Delnabo was home to a distillery in the 19th century, but the site was closed in 1858 and production moved to Glenlivet. Cross the bridge over the Avon, and turn right to climb the steep hill

opposite. The turning for the parking area at the start of the walk is on your right. If you are returning to Tomintoul on foot, simply continue on the road until you reach the village.

Map labels:
To Tomintoul
Delnabo House
Queen's Viewpoint
Water of Ailnack
Keppoch
River Avon
Delavorar
iron bridge
0 — 1km

Glenmulliach lookout

**Distance 6km Time 1 hour 30
Terrain forest tracks and paths; long
ascent, some steps and steep sections
Map OS Explorer OL58 Access no public
transport to the start**

**Follow a nature trail through the mixed
woodlands of Glenmulliach, before
climbing across heather moors to a
viewpoint overlooking Tomintoul and
the surrounding hills.**

Start from the Glenmulliach Forest car
park off the A939, just south of Tomintoul.
Glenmulliach is in the heart of the
Glenlivet Estate, owned by the Crown
since the land was acquired from the
Dukes of Gordon in the 1930s. The estate
has made great efforts to open up access
for walkers and cyclists, and this route
partly follows one of a number of
waymarked trails.

Walk up the track, ignoring the turning
off to the house at Glenmullie on the
right, and at the next junction turn right.
After another 300m, turn left and climb
uphill on a track.

Go through a gate to continue the
ascent and turn right at a T-junction to
pass a small pool used as a water reservoir
in case of forest fires. The track now
crosses open heather moorland. Look out
for the well-camoflagued mountain hares,
impressive in their white coats in winter
and brown in summer. Red grouse often
take flight from almost under your feet
when disturbed, with their distinctive
'go back' call. Turn right at the junction
and head towards a mast.

Before you get to the mast, you'll see a
viewpoint with bench and indicator on the
right. This is helpful to identify the hills,
farms and villages visible from here, with

Breac
Leathad   mast

viewpoint

◄ Looking towards Tomintoul from Glenmulliach viewpoint

the mountains rising behind. To the north
is an area where whisky smuggling was
once rife; there were frequent skirmishes
between smugglers and the
government's excise men. It is said
that more than 200 illicit stills
were worked in the area
known as the Braes
of Glenlivet.
Convoys of
Highland
ponies laden
with whisky
casks would set
out over the hills to
supply markets throughout
the northeast and beyond. To get the
whisky into the towns, it was often
decanted into a sheep's or calf's bladder
which could then be hidden under hats,
baskets of food or even women's skirts.

hide

To Tomintoul

A939

Glenmullie

Conglass Water

To Ballater

0   1km

From the viewpoint, retrace your steps
back to the track junction and turn left.
At the next junction keep straight on to
return on the north side of the Allt
Mulliach. After 500m turn right on a path
(SP Nature Trail) which heads into the
trees and eventually reaches a wooden
hide. The hide overlooks a glen where the
forestry has been thinned and, in some
places, cleared and replanted with native
species to try and increase the amount of
wildlife and flowers it can support.

After leaving the hide continue on the
path through the forest. The forest floor is
fantastic for fungi-foraging in late summer

and autumn, whilst spring is best for the
many small birds putting on vocal singing
contests in the hope of attracting a mate.
Regular visitors include siskin, common
crossbill, redwing and the improbably tiny
goldcrests. According to the estate, there is
a chance for the eagle-eyed – and very
lucky – to spy the elusive wildcat and pine
marten, but you are more likely to catch
sight of roe deer.

The path descends to a junction; turn
left here and continue heading downhill
alongside a fence at first and later in
zigzags to reach a footbridge. After this the
outward track is reached; turn right to
return to the parking area at the start.

The Livet Path

Distance 9.5km **Time** 3 hours
Terrain waymarked paths, tracks and
minor road, can be muddy in places
Map OS Explorer OL62 **Access** no public
transport to the start

Immerse yourself in the remote heather
moorland of the Glenlivet Estate on this
fine walk with opportunities to see
grouse, as well as curlews and lapwings
in the summer.

Take the minor road through
Tomnavoulin, passing the distillery, to
reach the parking area near Allanreid at
the end of the public road. (This route is
shown on the information board here
and waymarked as Walk 3.) Cross the
bridge and walk along the track below a
memorial cairn. Leave the track to go right
at a marker post and aim for the

footbridge, but don't cross; instead
continue on the grassy track which
heads upstream.

Follow the River Livet and carry on
along the track as it heads through a
forestry plantation. Once out of the trees
go through the gate to cross a pathless
field, keeping the fence on your left.
The track leads to another gate and is
joined by a track from the left before
crossing the burn and bearing right to
reach a wooden bridge.

After crossing the river, aim left to
continue up the glen on a track, passing
a lone cottage. Once past this final sign
of habitation the glen begins to take on a
remote feel, surrounded as it is by open
heather moorland.

In 1.5km, you reach a gate and stile –
turn right here to head uphill, sharing the

◄ The Livet Path

route next to the fence with the occasional mountain biker. In the 19th century this path would have been used by smugglers carrying whisky illegally distilled in the remote glens to traders who would sell it on. For a period the Livet area was a relatively safe haven for the distillers and smugglers, but that all changed with the arrival of notorious exciseman Malcolm Gillespie in the 1820s. Said to have been wounded some 42 times in skirmishes with smugglers, Gillespie kept a vicious black attack dog and was greatly feared by the outlaw community of stillmen.

Eventually King George IV granted a license to one stillman, George Smith, in 1824, who established the first legal distillery in Glenlivet. Considered a traitor by his old colleagues, however, he had to carry loaded pistols for protection in the early days. Today around six million bottles of The Glenlivet are sold every year, making it the second biggest selling whisky brand in the world.

Look out for a post indicating a right turn onto a track which is marked in places by stone cairns. There are good views to the Ladder Hills on the left. The track becomes rougher and boggy in places before coming to a stile; go over this and head to the left of a ruined house. After a gap in a fence the track leads to a gate; turn right here, crossing a field and aiming right when you reach the narrow point of the field to follow the path next to the fence aiming for the prominent Bochel hill ahead.

Keep to the right of two farmhouses and then cross the stile at the end of the field, joining the Bochel circuit (waymarked as Walk 10). Keep straight ahead as the path crosses rough grassland until you meet another gate where you leave the Bochel circuit. Climb the stile and head to the left of the farmhouse to another stile. From here pick up the track which winds downhill to the footbridge passed earlier. Cross this and bear left to follow the outward track back to the start.

The magnificent River Dee winds its sweeping course through one of Scotland's most beautiful glens. The heavily wooded slopes are backed by wild and remote mountains, with mighty Lochnagar towering over its lesser neighbours. Queen Victoria fell in love with this area and, when she bought Balmoral Castle and Estate, it became one of Britain's most fashionable retreats for the wealthy. Today, the Royal Family still returns every year –

joined by many other holiday visitors.

Ballater is at the heart of the region, having rapidly expanded around the railway which arrived here in 1866. Many of Europe's heads of state passed through the station in the late-19th century. The railway line has sadly gone, but Ballater's attractive streets are packed with independent shops bearing the Royal insignia and the words 'By Appointment'. The appeal of the town remains just as strong.

Knock Castle near Ballater ▶

Ballater and Royal Deeside

Glen Tanar and the drove roads

Distance 8km Time 2 hours 30
Terrain **waymarked paths and tracks**
Map **OS Explorer OL54**
Access **no public transport**

Experience the splendour of the natural pine forest that cloaks Glen Tanar. Among the varied wildlife that make this National Nature Reserve their home are red squirrels, crested tits, crossbills and the rare capercaillie.

The walk starts from the Braeloine car park (fee) on the right-hand side of the minor road up Glen Tanar. Begin by crossing the very beautiful humpback Bridge of Tanar. The building on the far side to the left is the estate's visitor centre, with a wealth of information about the countryside and a ranger on duty most days. This walk is the longest of several waymarked trails and follows the green markers, heading upstream away from the visitor centre by a track.

This track soon leaves the river and swings to the left to pass the tiny Chapel of Lesmo, built in 1872 by the eccentric Manchester MP Sir William Cunliffe Brooks. The chapel, whose pews are lined with deerskin, is usually kept locked. Just beyond it, you come to a T-junction, where you turn right and head directly across a larger track and into the woods.

This part of the route follows the line of the Firmounth, an old right of way over the mountains to Glen Esk in Angus. The track climbs to The Knockie viewpoint – the name coming from the Gaelic *cnoc*, meaning 'rock', where a bench gives a wonderful view up the glen. The trees here have been replanted since the Second World War, but the view ahead reveals a wide sweep of original Caledonian pinewood stretching across the glen. Turn right, heading downhill to join and bear left up the track along the floor of the glen. Further on, the route passes an

◄ Path through the woodland

elaborately housed spring, also built by Cunliffe Brooks, and then crosses a small bridge over the Burn of Skinna. Continue over the much larger old stone bridge which spans the Water of Allachy. On the far side, turn right and accompany the main track, ignoring an uphill branch to the left, to cross another bridge, this time over the Tanar itself. You now come to the old Mounth Road, another historic drove route over the hills, at a T-junction. Turn right to begin the walk back down the far side of the glen, steering close to the river and past a semi-derelict stone shed.

Eventually, you reach a signed junction, where the the main track curves left, signed for Aboyne and Dinnet. Don't go this way; instead follow the waymarked trail off to the right, passing a fenced forest lochan with a boathouse on the far side. The track continues to Knockie Bridge, which you cross and turn left on the far side.

Soon after, you go straight over a track coming in from the right (on the left it reaches a locked bridge over the Tanar) to traverse a grassy field and run close to the river, with a beautiful stone estate cottage on the far bank. On this

section, you'll see some particularly fine Scots pines. To the right, a fenced granite millstone is all that now remains of a watermill. The strange conical building here used to house a turbine. When you emerge onto a track, continue ahead to return to the visitor centre and old Bridge of Tanar.

The Vat return

Distance 6.5km **Time** 2 hours
Terrain waymarked paths, some steep
sections; optional rough clamber into the
Vat on stepping stones **Map** OS Explorer
OL59 **Access** bus to Dinnet where a path
can be followed via Loch Kinord

**Hidden in the forests of the Muir of
Dinnet is the Vat, an amazing natural
amphitheatre accessed through a narrow
gap and once a hiding place for
vagabonds and outlaws. The walk
continues on a woodland climb with
grand views.**

Begin from the Burn o'Vat car park off
the Ballater to Aboyne road. There is a
visitor centre here, giving information
about the Vat and the surrounding area.
Pass the front of the visitor centre and to
the left of the toilet block. The path is
identified by purple waymarkers as it
descends gently, bears right and then
crosses a wooden bridge before heading
upstream. Carry straight on, leaving the

waymarkers for the short detour into the
Vat and ignoring a second bridge on the
right. It looks as though the way ahead is
blocked by large rocks, but here is the
hidden entrance to the Vat, a gigantic
water-gouged bowl. To enter, follow the
burn, using the stepping stones to keep to
the right-hand side. This section may be
impassable when the burn is in spate, and
care should be taken as the rocks can be
slippery. Once inside, the true scale of the
Vat can be appreciated as humans look
tiny against the overhanging walls of rock

The Vat was carved from the stone by
the action of raging glacial meltwaters at
the end of the last ice age. It became a
popular attraction in Victorian times, but
before then was a hiding place for
fugitives. In the 17th century, after the civil
war, gangs of looters roamed the
countryside plundering local crops,
livestock and valuables. The local farmers
paid one Gilderoy MacGregor who,
together with his men, acted as protector

◂ Footpath above the Vat

and dealt with the looters. However, once the disturbances were over, Gilderoy set up a cattle-rustling scheme himself using the old drove routes. He is believed to have used the cave in the Vat as a hiding place for a number of years. A proclamation was issued in 1636 calling for Gilderoy's capture, with a reward offered of £1000 dead or alive. He was eventually caught and hanged in 1658. The cave is behind the waterfall: it is impossible to access it without getting wet.

After exploring the Vat, return along the path to the bridge. This time, cross it and make the steep ascent up the path beyond, turning left at a waymarked junction to continue your climb through the trees. At the top, turn right to follow the sign for the Culbein Circular. The route now passes through more open heather-clad ground, before dropping through the pinewoods.

Eventually, you come to a surfaced track. A right turn here takes you to the main road, which you cross, turning right to follow a path running alongside it. After passing a farm and house on the right, go through a gap in a stone wall, then bear left into a birchwood. An obvious path weaves its way through the lovely woods, with views

of Loch Davan to your left. This area is part of the Muir of Dinnet National Nature Reserve and is home to a variety of wildlife, including a large gaggle of overwintering geese.

Follow the green posts, turning right at a clear junction marked with both red and green. Turn right again at the next path junction before emerging in a small parking area. Cross this to take the path which runs parallel with the road, then heads left into the trees. Soon the path reaches a junction beside the road: turn right to cross the road and return to the visitor centre.

69

Wild side of Loch Kinord

Distance 6km Time 2 hours
Terrain mostly level woodland paths
Map OS Explorer OL59 Access bus to
Dinnet, where you'll find a path leading
to the far end of Loch Kinord

This waymarked trail makes a beautiful
circuit of lovely Loch Kinord in the Muir of
Dinnet National Nature Reserve. The walk
is excellent for both watching birds on
the loch and spotting other wildlife in the
birch woodland.

Start from the Burn o'Vat car park off the
Ballater to Aboyne road. Details of several
waymarked routes, as well as local geology
and wildlife, can be found in the visitor
centre. This walk follows the blue and
white duck waymarkers, crossing the main
road to reach a T-junction with a path.
Turn right here and walk through the
lovely birchwoods which, along with the
loch itself, are part of the Muir of Dinnet
National Nature Reserve. The luxuriant
lichen blanketing many of the trees is

evidence of the purity of the air here. Cross
a small footbridge and then a track to
continue alongside a stone wall.

There are a couple of small lochans in
the woods, ideal for spotting dragonflies
in summer. When the path starts to rise
towards a little chapel at Meikle Kinord,
bear left to reach the shore of the loch.
Like neighbouring Loch Davan, Kinord is
an example of a kettlehole, a loch
occupying a shallow basin scooped out
during the last ice age.

Keeping with the waymarkers, go
through a gap in a drystone dyke and then
over a wooden footbridge. At the junction
beyond, turn left through the trees, twice
passing through further gaps in
tumbledown walls. At one point, the path
swings to the right through a gate before
heading back down to the enchanting
lochside. This is a popular spot for
whooper swans, greylag geese and wigeon,
which spend the winter months here. In
the summer, you may see ospreys fishing

◄ Lochan in Muir of Dinnet National Nature Reserve

as they have recolonised the area since the early 1980s, and the loch is also an important feeding place for otters.

At a wooden signpost, look left across the water to a small island. This is all that remains of a crannog, a defensive Iron Age dwelling built on wooden piles driven into the bed of the loch. According to local legend, this one was used as a prison by the laird of a nearby castle. Stay by the water to go through a small gate, before bearing right uphill away from the loch. Soon the path reaches an intricately carved stone cross, almost 2m high and enclosed by a fence. This is a Pictish symbol stone, a beautiful 9th-century relic.

When the path joins a grassy track, turn left through birch trees, thereafter swinging left and then right to follow the waymarkers. After going straight across a turning area, the path leads you to a wooden signpost where you turn right and later join a larger track. Just before this reaches the road, switch left and then right as the Burn o'Vat car park and visitor centre come into view.

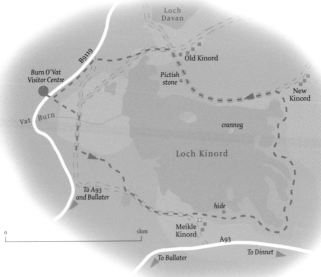

Seven Bridges and Knock Castle

Distance 10.5km Time 3 hours
Terrain **waymarked paths and tracks**
Maps OS Explorer OL59 and OL53
Access **Ballater is well served by buses**

**Ballater is a compact little town of fine
stone-built villas, and is proud of its
Royal connections. This circular walk
explores the delightful countryside
around it, centring on the River Dee and
crossing seven bridges along the way.**

Start at the attractive former railway
station, often used by Queen Victoria and
now a visitor centre, in the heart of
Ballater. Follow the A93 for Braemar over
the old bridge, built to cross the railway
extension to Braemar: this line was never
completed as Queen Victoria objected to
trains passing Balmoral. Just before a
converted church with prominent spire,
turn left into Invercauld Road and then
next right (waymarked) to access a path:
this goes straight over a crossroads.

At the edge of an oakwood, take the
right fork past a wooden barrier. This is
the start of a delightful woodland section
as the path follows the planned line of the
never-completed railway above the River
Dee. The slopes fall away steeply in places:
at one point, known as Postie's Leap, the
path crosses a dramatic gorge by a bridge.

Soon leaving the woods and river
behind, your route forks up the slope
on the right, passing a wooden house to
head towards the A93. Before reaching the
main road, fork left past sheds to reach a
track at the far end of the farm and turn
right to cross a footbridge over the
River Gairn. Follow the path as it bears left
and then aims to the right to follow the
River Dee upstream. Keep left near a gate
to return to the riverside at Polhollick
Bridge, an elegant white suspension
footbridge (1892).

On the other side, a track leads you left
into Dalliefour Wood, a Scots pine

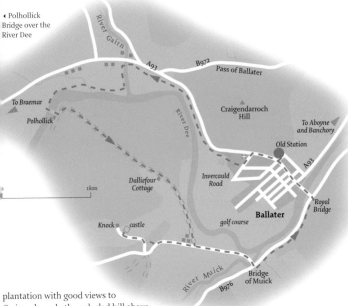

◂ Polhollick Bridge over the River Dee

plantation with good views to Craigendarroch, the oak-clad hill above Ballater. The cottage on your right was once home to a renowned angler and poacher who, according to his own calculations, lived to be 124.

In about 1km, you come to a road. To detour to Knock Castle, a 16th-century towerhouse with a grisly history, go right for 400m, leaving the road where it bends left for the rough track that goes straight up into the wood. Ignoring a branch-off on the right, climb to a bigger stony track with a first glimpse of Knock Castle. Turn right and, once level with the castle, access it across a stile and field. The elevated position gives the castle fine views over lush countryside. Return to the road where you joined it, then follow it over the Bridge of Muick at Bridgend Cottages, staying on the main road (left) and crossing a bridge over the small Brackley Burn to accompany the stately Dee once more. Further on, turn left over the Royal Bridge, opened by Queen Victoria in 1885: it had several predecessors, all of which succumbed to the might of the Dee in full flood. Walk along the main street of Ballater to return to the Old Royal Station.

Craigendarroch oakwoods

Distance **4km** Time **2 hours**
Terrain **waymarked paths; steep sections,
steps** Map **OS Explorer OL59 or OL53**
Access **Ballater is well served by buses**

**Craigendarroch may be a small hill, but
it has a big place in the affections of
Ballater folk. Reaching the summit
requires a very steep climb through the
oakwoods, but the views from the top are
a fantastic reward.**

Begin from the former railway station in
the centre of Ballater. Follow the A93
towards Braemar, passing fine stone-built
villas and the Auld Kirk on the opposite
side. A footpath sign indicates a right turn
onto Craigendarroch Walk, where you
soon branch left onto a path into the
oakwoods. The path slopes up to the right
behind the houses – turn left at the red
marker post – before making the steep
zigzag climb between fine old oak trees.
Above this section, the ascent is more
gradual and the path contours the slopes
to the left. Craigendarroch is a National
Nature Reserve, famed for its fine oak
trees: until the 18th century, these were
coppiced and the wood used to make
cartwheels. After about 300m, you meet a
signed junction. The path ahead makes a
complete circuit of Craigendarroch, an
attractive alternative to this route, but to
stick with the signed walk described here,
turn right for the summit.

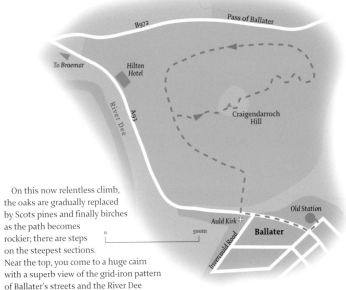

On this now relentless climb, the oaks are gradually replaced by Scots pines and finally birches as the path becomes rockier; there are steps on the steepest sections. Near the top, you come to a huge cairn with a superb view of the grid-iron pattern of Ballater's streets and the River Dee flowing sedately beyond. Opposite, you'll see a steep, forested hill with a mast: this is Craig Coillich, the objective for the hill race during the local Highland Games.

Just beyond is the true summit of Craigendarroch, with a bench and an indicator to help identify the mountains in view in all directions. If the weather is clear then the northern cliffs of Lochnagar look particularly striking, towering above its more rounded foothills.

To continue the walk, follow the path past a red marker and begin the steep descent down the far side. Turn left at a junction and soon you'll see the crags

across the Pass of Ballater. The path descends in a series of switchbacks before levelling off. The pass was formed along the line of a natural fault and carved out in the ice age by a glacier. Today, it carries a road that bypasses Ballater. Both sides of the pass are surprisingly steep, so take care of the drop on your right.

The pines soon give way to oaks once more as the slope eases and the path passes a couple of benches. When you meet the junction where you turned up the hill earlier, go straight ahead and retrace your steps to the start of the walk and the centre of the town.

◀ Craigendarroch from Ballater

75

Royal visit to Loch Muick

Distance 12.5km **Time** 3 hours 30
Terrain Good paths, tracks
Map OS Explorer OL53
Access no public transport

This classic circuit around Loch Muick takes you into the wilder parts of the Balmoral Estate below majestic Lochnagar. The walk is fairly easy going, passing an impressive lodge built for Queen Victoria and still used as a retreat by the Royal Family today. Large herds of red deer are a frequent sight.

Begin the walk from the Balmoral Estate Visitor Centre at the Spittal of Glenmuick, 10km up the glen on a minor road off the B976. The centre is well worth a visit for its informative displays on the local wildlife, flora and the history of the estate, and it is staffed by knowledgeable rangers. Leave the car park (fee), pass the centre and a vehicle barrier, then turn right onto a track which crosses the floor of the glen and the River Muick en route

to the houses at Allt-an-guibhsaich, meaning 'River of the Pines' in Gaelic. When you reach the first building here, turn left onto another track. The path to the right is the usual access for Lochnagar, the highest mountain in the area and hugely popular with hillwalkers and mountaineers all year round.

Continue straight ahead below the lodge to reach Loch Muick by a pretty stone boathouse. Here, a path crossing the foot of the loch can be used as a picturesque shortcut back to the start if there isn't time for the full circuit. Otherwise, keep to the elevated track as it skirts the side of the loch, passing a fenced area on the left. The fence excludes deer in an attempt to allow natural regeneration of the forest to occur. Eventually, you'll see the stone wall and pines surrounding Glas-allt Shiel ahead. This fine lodge was built by Queen Victoria after the death of Prince Albert. She used it frequently as a quiet retreat

◂ Red deer on the track at Loch Muick

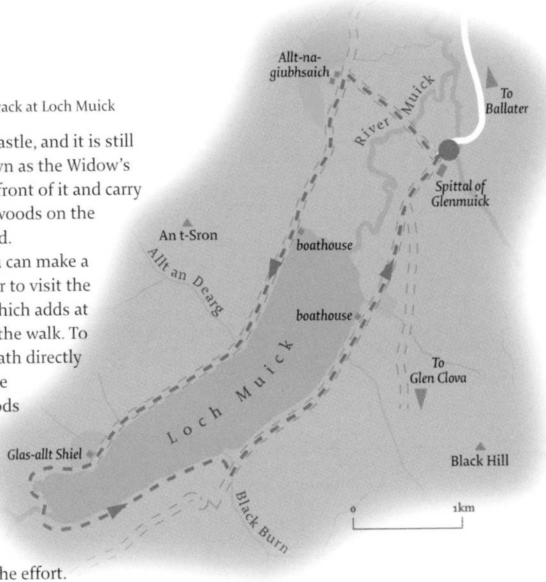

Allt-na-giubhsaich

River Muick

To Ballater

Spittal of Glenmuick

An t-Sron

boathouse

Allt an Dearg

boathouse

To Glen Clova

Loch Muick

Glas-allt Shiel

Black Hill

Black Burn

0   1km

from Balmoral Castle, and it is still sometimes known as the Widow's House. Pass the front of it and carry on through the woods on the clear path beyond.

From here, you can make a strenuous detour to visit the Glas Allt Falls, which adds at least an hour to the walk. To do so, take the path directly behind the house through the woods for a steep, and in places difficult, climb. In fine weather, and especially after heavy rain, it is well worth the effort.

Continuing the circuit of the loch, the path emerges from the pines which shelter the house before the head of the loch comes into view. Keep left at a fork and follow the water's edge. The path crosses a number of small wooden bridges and passes some sandy beaches which make for tempting rest stops. Once round the head of the loch, the path becomes more distinct as it weaves through the heather. After a while, it climbs up to join a vehicle track at a bridge. Turn left here, crossing the bridge to accompany the track as it slopes back alongside the water. There are great views across to the Glas-allt Shiel lodge visited earlier. Look out also for large herds of red deer that frequent this area.

During the summer months, you may see adders basking on the path and also the rare ring ouzel – sometimes known as the 'blackbird of the moors'.

Looking back, the distinctive shape of Broad Cairn, classed as one of the 284 Scottish Munros or mountains over 3000ft (914m), can be seen above the head of the loch. After passing a more modern boathouse, the track merges with a route coming in from Glen Clova. Keep straight ahead, passing Loch-end Wood, which once sheltered another hunting lodge, long since demolished. Further on, the woods and buildings at the Spittal of Glenmuick come into view and it is a short walk back to the start.

77

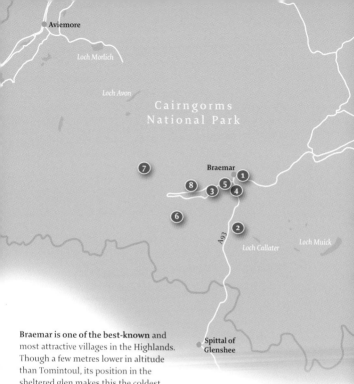

Aviemore

Loch Morlich

Loch Avon

Cairngorms
National Park

Braemar

⑦ ⑧ ③ ⑤ ①
          ④
    ⑥
              ②

A93

Loch Callater   Loch Muick

Spittal of
Glenshee

Braemar is one of the best-known and most attractive villages in the Highlands. Though a few metres lower in altitude than Tomintoul, its position in the sheltered glen makes this the coldest place in Britain: the record temperature of -27°C was recorded here in the winter of 1982. Braemar has a long history: the 1000-year-old remains of its original castle are in the village centre, whilst today's impressive keep to the north dates only from a comparatively recent 1628. The village is famed for the Braemar Gathering – the local Highland Games – which is attended by members of the Royal Family in September each year.

Braemar is the perfect centre from which to explore the stunning landscape of the Upper Dee. Wild glens penetrate deep into the surrounding mountains, giving the walker a chance to wander amongst pine and birchwoods, isolated lochs and thundering waterfalls. The abundance of wildlife and the feeling of being on the very edge of the vast roadless mountain wilderness of the central Cairngorms cannot be matched.

Invercauld House near Braemar ▶

The Braes of Mar

Keiloch Crag and the Fog House

Distance 5km **Time** 2 hours
Terrain clear paths, tracks
Map OS Explorer OL58 **Access** bus from
Aberdeen and Braemar stops at entrance
to driveway on A93

**This circular walk on the Invercauld
Estate climbs a crag overlooking the River
Dee. It passes a heather-thatched 'fog
house' with good views on the way.
A great walk for spotting birds of prey
such as buzzards or even golden eagles.**

Just off the A93 at Keiloch, between
Crathie and Braemar, there is a signed
walkers' car park on the Invercauld
Estate (fee). This has been in the ownership of
the Farquharson family for almost 600
years, and is a traditional sporting estate
with income from deer-stalking, forestry,
tourism and fishing. The current owner,
Captain Alwyne Farquharson of
Invercauld, is the 16th laird and chieftain
of the clan, and the estate welcomes

walkers. This extends to the decor in the
toilet at the car park which is wallpapered
with back issues of *The Angry Corrie*, the
much-missed hillwalkers' fanzine.

This is the shorter of two waymarked
circuits. Begin along the tarmac
continuation of the road into the car park,
signed as a public footpath to the Linn of
Quoich. It passes some attractive estate
cottages and, if the weather is clear, gives
fine views to Beinn a'Bhuird, one of the
most remote of the Cairngorms
mountains, in the distance ahead.

The road continues through woodland
along a fine avenue of mature beech trees.
Soon, the back of Invercauld House comes
into view through the trees. Just before
the house, turn right where a wooden
sign for Craig Leek points uphill. The
name originates from the Gaelic *Creag
Leacach*, meaning 'Slabby Crag', but this
route passes beneath the rocks on the
lower wooded slopes.

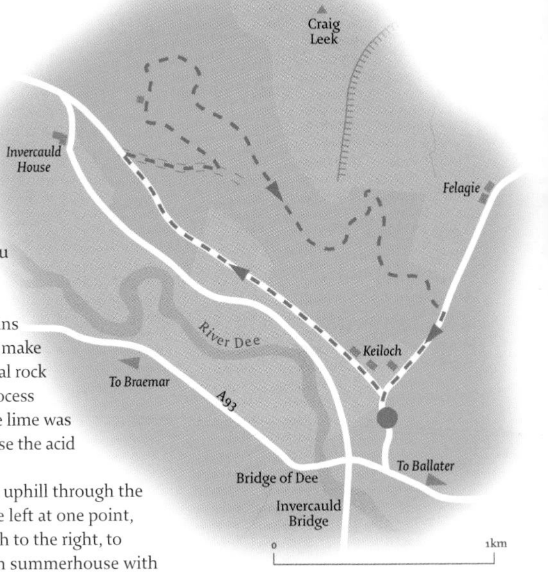

◄ Snow-clad
Beinn a'Bhuird
from near Keiloch

At the next
junction, turn right
and let the purple
waymarkers guide you
on a rising course
through the forest.
This passes the remains
of a limekiln, built to make
fertiliser from the local rock
through a heating process
known as slaking; the lime was
then used to neutralise the acid
soils nearby.

As the path snakes uphill through the
woods, it turns to the left at one point,
ignoring another path to the right, to
reach a small wooden summerhouse with
an excellent outlook over the Dee below.
It is known as the Fog House as the roof is
thatched with heather, which is known
locally as 'fog'. Built by the estate as a
folly, it was to be the first of several
planned fog houses, but construction of
the others never went ahead. Immediately
after the Fog House, bear right uphill for a
steep ascent to a metal gate where the
path starts to level off.

The route now bears right to traverse
the side of the hill, with views across the
River Dee to Ballochbuie Forest and the
White Mouth plateau beyond. According
to Adam Watson in the Scottish
Mountaineering Club classic *The
Cairngorms*, local legend has it that 'when

ye White Mouth frae snow is clear, ye
day of doom is drawing near' – perhaps a
foretelling of global warming. Buzzards
are commonly seen here, circling on the
thermals, and sightings of golden eagles
are possible too. Continue straight ahead
at a junction, and keep following the wide
track as it curves round Craig Leek and
towards the open countryside.

Soon, the small red estate house at
Felagie can be seen in the distance. The
track descends by a couple of wide loops
before joining the track from Felagie. Turn
right along this track which leads past a
collection of estate buildings and back to
the car park.

On Jock's Road to Loch Callater

Distance 11.5km **Time** 3 hours 30
Terrain good track, narrow path by loch
Map OS Explorer OL60 **Access** no public
transport but Braemar is a 3.5km walk
from the start point

Follow a track up to lonely Loch Callater, enclosed by high mountains and a wonderful spot for a summer's picnic.

The walk starts from a parking area (charge) on the A93 south of Braemar, just south of the bridge over the Callater Burn and Auchallater Farm. Take the track, signed as a right of way to Glen Clova, up a gentle incline. The signpost is a reminder of an important public access battle in the late- 19th century over this traditional cattle-droving route. The Glen Doll Estate had been purchased by the wealthy Duncan MacPherson on his return from time in Australia. He immediately blocked access across his land, drawing protests from the access movement, including one John (Jock) Winter who defied the ban. A party from the Scottish Rights of Way Society walked across the estate, putting up rights of way signs in direct opposition to MacPherson. They were stopped at the far end by his gamekeepers. A mighty court battle ensued and, although the House of Lords eventually ruled in favour of public access in 1888, the lengthy action bankrupted both MacPherson and the Rights of Way Society. However, the action led to the passing of the Scottish Rights of Way Act, the most important piece of legislation for walkers until the more recent Land Reform Act of 2003 gave Scotland some of the most progressive access laws in Europe.

Go through a gate to accompany the cascading Callater Burn on a track that rises gently through the heather-clad lower glen. Ignoring a branch to the right, you eventually cross the burn by a bridge. Keep on the main track, disregarding another fork to the right, until you see the buildings of Lochcallater Lodge in front of you. As you approach the lodge, the track

To Braemar
Auchallater
A93
Sron
Dubh
To Spittal of
Glenshee
Callater Burn
1km
Loch
Phadruig
Glen Callater
Callater
Stable
Lochcallater
Lodge
Loch Callater
To
Lochnagar
Jock's Road to
Glen Clova

Today, the crags around Loch Callater are home to the rare ring ouzel. Slightly smaller than a blackbird, the males have a striking white band around their neck and breast, making them easy to identify – although they are notoriously shy. The loch itself is popular for pike fishing.

After exploring the side of the loch, retrace your steps down the glen to the start. In very dry weather, the walk can be extended with a complete circuit of the loch (add 1 hour 30), but this entails a river crossing: there is no bridge. Though

branches again: keep left to follow it through the gate and between two buildings. The main building was originally a lodge for deerstalking parties. The small stable on the left is now a walkers' shelter, maintained by volunteers from the Mountain Bothies Association.

To reach the loch, cross a stile ahead. The walk can be extended by taking the path to the left along the shore: this passes some small, sandy stretches with superb mountain views across the water. The route of Jock's Road climbs up and over the great plateau to the left of Tolmount, the prominent conical mountain set back from the head of the glen. Even in good weather, the Mounth plateau is exceptionally exposed, and Jock's Road has been the site of a number of tragedies caused by poor weather, most notably when five men died during a snowstorm on New Year's Day in 1959.

straightforward after a dry spell – it usually involves a short wade – it would be dangerous when the river is in spate.

On the way back, look out for a stone marking the Priest's Well and, according to legend, the site of a miracle. The story is that Braemar was gripped by a particularly extreme winter, causing the well near Lochcallater Lodge to freeze solid, leaving the villages with no supply of drinking water. The clergyman was called in and began praying at the well. As he knelt and started his prayers the ice began to melt and a thaw set in.

Morrone Birkwood

Distance 4.5km **Time** 2 hours
Terrain waymarked paths and tracks with
some ascent **Map** OS Explorer OL60
Access bus from Aberdeen

Birk is Scots for birch and Morrone
Birkwood is one of the finest natural
birchwoods remaining in the UK.
A fine circular walk explores this
remarkable and atmospheric place with
its twisted, lichen-draped trees and
dense juniper stands. The views of the
mountains are superb.

There is a car park at the top of Chapel
Brae in Braemar at the start of the walk,
but it is just as straightforward to begin
from the village centre. Take the Linn of
Dee road and turn left at the small
roundabout towards the west end of the
village, immediately keeping right at the
fork. The car park is on the left, near the
top of the public road. Continue up the
road and then the track, passing an
attractive duck pond backed by the slopes
of Morrone. From here, the route is
waymarked in blue: take a left at the fork.

At the signposted junction, keep to the
left, the track winding left and right as it
climbs up into the birchwoods. The varied
and very heavy growth of lichen hanging
from the branches is evidence of the lack
of air pollution here. It gives these woods
a feeling of great age, an impression that
has been verified by pollen analysis

showing that the vegetation here has not changed since the last ice age. Beneath the trees is a dense underlayer of juniper bushes. Pass the farmhouse of Woodhill and at the fork head left uphill on a path which leads to a viewpoint and bench, a good place to pause and admire the fine views back across the birch trees and the Dee.

Turn right onto a track at the junction just beyond the viewpoint. The most strenuous part of the route is over as the path now leads across the birch-clad slopes. Pass through a gate, the fence here protecting the most important part of the woods from being damaged by red deer. Beyond, the trees thin out, allowing more open views. The cone of Derry Cairngorm dominates the distant skyline, covered by snow until well into spring whilst, over to the right, Braemar nestles amidst a carpet of fields and forests, backed by sweeping hills.

Now the path reaches a plantation at a stile. Do not cross this, but instead turn right and keep to the path on the near side of the fence. Soon it curves to the right and heads into the birchwood, marking the start of the return walk to Braemar. Ignore another path coming in from the left and continue, crossing two small burns before reaching the fenced part of the woods again. Keep to the left of the fence to reach a track which leads you back to the outward route. From here, retrace your steps to Chapel Brae and the village.

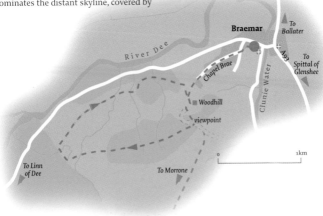

◂ The River Dee from Morrone Birkwood

The Lion's Face and the Cromlins

Distance 5.5km Time 2 hours 30
Terrain waymarked paths; initial rough
and poorly marked climb through woods
Map OS Explorer OL57 Access bus from
Aberdeen

This varied circuit from Braemar takes in
pinewoods, cliffs and fields with several
excellent viewpoints. Braemar Castle can
be visited along the way.

Begin from the centre of Braemar where
there is a car park and public toilets.
Facing the Fife Arms, the large hotel
opposite the tourist information centre,
turn right to head back up to the main
A93. Cross this and turn right briefly,
looking out for a wooden signpost which
points you down a lane alongside the
church. Leave this lane when it curves to
the right after 300m, and go straight
ahead into the woods via a large gate. In
the woods, bear right at a fingerpost sign

and follow the yellow waymarkers. When
the path forks again, keep on the larger
route to the left.

As you continue the climb through the
woods, stay on the main path and ignore
branches off to the right. After a fair
amount of ascent, the path cuts across the
slope to the right and passes through a
gap in a tumbledown drystone dyke. Bear
right here to emerge from the trees at a
wooden signpost. The piles of stones here
are all that remains of a cottage which was
once the home of Mr and Mrs Thompson.
They were relatives of John Brown, Queen
Victoria's famous servant, and he often
brought the Queen here bearing gifts of
tobacco and tea. The wide path that
descends right, still known as the Queen's
Drive, makes a fine walk in its own right,
leading to the A93 which can then be
followed back to Braemar. For the Lion's
Face, however, turn left on a beautifully

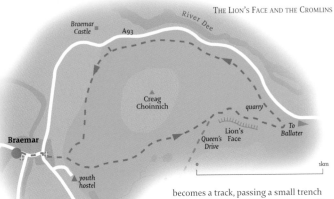

constructed path, soon with views towards the striking granite tors on the summit of remote Ben Avon.

A little further on, there's an even better viewpoint at a bench. Ahead, the River Dee and its pastures make a beautiful setting for the castle-like Invercauld House, still the private home of the Farquharson family, though various enterprises are run from the estate.

The path now passes below the large rocky crag known as the Lion's Face: although the resemblance is only obvious from across the Dee; these days, the trees make a clear view difficult. Beyond the Lion's Face, the path begins to slope downhill, going over a small burn by a bridge and then crossing back again. As you approach a small quarry, head right towards a gate onto the A93, but turn left just before meeting it to follow a rough path in the adjacent woods. After the quarry, this starts to rise and briefly

becomes a track, passing a small trench constructed by Braemar's Home Guard in World War Two. It then descends and goes through another gate, close to the A93.

Turn left uphill to continue the walk, or go right and then cross the road to detour to Braemar Castle. Recently leased by the Invercauld Estate to the local community, the castle has undergone extensive restoration and is once again open to the public. Opening times can be found at the tourist information centre in Braemar.

Back across the road, the route climbs beside the fence to reach a fine viewpoint for the Cromlins, looking across to Braemar and the upper Dee, where an indicator helps identify the many distant summits seen on a clear day. Keep to the path to cross a large stile and re-enter the larch forest. Carefully follow the yellow markers along a rough path until you come to a junction. If you're feeling energetic, it is possible to turn left here for the steep ascent to Creag Choinnich and even better views, though the climb is quite strenuous. Otherwise, turn right to take the path back down to Braemar.

◀ Braemar Castle

Dee tour from Braemar

Distance 5km **Time** 1 hour 30
Terrain rough but waymarked paths,
short climb near end **Map** OS Explorer
OL58 **Access** bus from Aberdeen

Braemar, one of the highest villages in
Britain, has a long and distinguished
history – which accounts for some of its
appeal to visitors. Its magnificent
surroundings are explored on this
straightforward circuit, taking in serene
riverbanks and spellbinding views.

Start the walk from the public car park
off the main A93, almost opposite the
Invercauld Arms. From here, cross the
River Clunie on a wooden footbridge and
turn right to follow a narrow path
alongside the riverbank. After sweeping
around a graceful arc in the river, you'll
see the keep of Braemar Castle over to the
right. The castle, which was built in 1628

by the then Earl of Mar, was recently
leased to the local community, who have
embarked on an ambitious restoration
project and re-opened it to the public.

Keep to the riverbank as you pass a small
sewage works and go through a wooden
gate. After running along the top of a stone
embankment, the path reaches the
confluence of the Clunie with the larger
River Dee. Some fine specimens of Scots
pine can be seen on the far side, enhancing
what is already a beautiful spot. The path
now turns sharp left and shadows the Dee
upstream, where on a clear day you'll have
fine views of the main mass of the mighty
Cairngorms straight ahead, before briefly
parting company with the river and
returning to it as it curves round. The
Braemar to Linn of Dee road can be seen
above you here.

Still on the path close to the river, head

◀ The village of Braemar

towards a large white house, passing below the grounds and then climbing left to meet the road: a signpost marks the way. Go over the stile and cross the road before taking the track directly opposite.

The route now heads quite steeply uphill to soon reach a bench with good views over the upper Dee. After passing through an area of scrubby birch trees, and just before a gate, turn left to continue alongside a fenced enclosure to a track at the top of Chapel Brae. Take this road downhill, past a duck pond and car park on the right and then houses on either side.

About halfway down on the right is the venue for the Braemar Gathering. This is the most famous of all Highland Games, and is usually attended by the Queen and other members of the Royal Family. Held on the first Saturday in September, it can attract crowds of more than 18,000. The origins of the Games are thought to date back to the 11th century when it was traditional at this time of year for clan chiefs to gather their men together for a huge

deer hunt lasting several days. During this time, competitions would be held to find the strongest, quickest and most skilful warriors. In the evening, storytelling and piping contests entertained the gathering.

At the bottom of the hill, turn right to follow the main street past the community hall and back into the centre of Braemar. To return to the start of the walk, continue past the wonderful Fife Arms building and over the bridge – looking out for the waterfalls – before turning left to reach the Invercauld Arms and the car park opposite.

89

The Colonel's Bed from Inverey

Distance **5km** Time **1 hour 30**
Terrain **vehicle track, then a rough path;**
take care by the gorge Map **OS Explorer**
OL60 Access **no public transport**

Visit the Colonel's Bed, a chasm where
the River Ey gushes though a cleft in the
rocks. Once the hiding place of an
outlawed colonel, the 'Bed' makes a
dramatic objective for this short walk
from the attractive hamlet of Inverey
near Braemar.

There is a car park in Meikle Inverey,
which is the larger part of Inverey on the
east side of the river, 'Meikle' being Scots
for large. The far side is known as Little
Inverey. Start out on the track signed for

Glen Ey, slanting uphill. The grey granite
memorial commemorates the life of John
Lamont, an astronomer who was born at
Corriemulzie, not far from Inverey. On a
clear day, there are great views to the right
over Ben Macdui and Derry Cairngorm.

Soon the track passes through the
grounds of Inverey House, before leaving
through a gate and continuing up the
glen. After a short while, cross the Ey Burn
on a wooden bridge and follow the track
as it climbs steeply at first. About 1km on,
where the track bends to the right, look
for the small wooden sign marked 'Col
Bed' – it's close to the ground and easily
missed – and join the narrow path to the
left here. The first section is an old

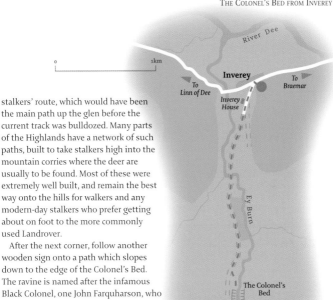

stalkers' route, which would have been the main path up the glen before the current track was bulldozed. Many parts of the Highlands have a network of such paths, built to take stalkers high into the mountain corries where the deer are usually to be found. Most of these were extremely well built, and remain the best way onto the hills for walkers and any modern-day stalkers who prefer getting about on foot to the more commonly used Landrover.

After the next corner, follow another wooden sign onto a path which slopes down to the edge of the Colonel's Bed. The ravine is named after the infamous Black Colonel, one John Farquharson, who took part in the first Jacobite rebellion of November 1688 in resistance to the rule of William of Orange who had seized the throne. One of his more famous escapades was the burning of Braemar Castle to prevent a force of more than 100 government troops from occupying and using it as a base. In 1689, he took part in the Battle of Killiecrankie where the Jacobites' leader John Graham was killed. After the battle the Black Colonel returned to his home at Inverey Castle, but as a wanted man he was forced to go into hiding. He chose a deep rock shelf hidden in the gorge as his hide-out and, although government troops plundered and burnt down his castle, retainers and

supporters provided him with food until his death of old age in 1698.

The path is rough, and you should take great care as you approach the Bed. The river flows through a sheer-sided rocky gorge here, and any fall into the unprotected depths would be fatal. The colonel's shelter no longer exists following the collapse of part of the gorge wall; any descent into the gorge today would be extremely dangerous and is not recommended. Instead, enjoy the spot from above before retracing your steps to Inverey.

◀ Track to Glen Ey

Linn of Dee to Derry Lodge

Distance 11km Time 3 hours
Terrain **clear, level paths and tracks**
Map **OS Explorer OL58 or OL57**
Access **no public transport**

This walk runs from the picturesque Linn of Dee to Derry Lodge, a Victorian deerstalkers' base, now derelict but with a wonderful setting in Glen Derry. The route gives a real flavour of the wild character of the glens running deep into the Cairngorms range.

The walk starts from the Linn of Dee car park (fee). Hardened hillwalkers use this as the starting point for expeditions into the highest mountains of the Cairngorms, as well as for the through route to Aviemore via the Lairig Ghru. Before setting out, head back over the road to visit the Linn itself. The River Dee runs through a narrow, rocky gorge, forcing the

water to cascade into a bubbling mass below. The bridge over the gorge was built in Victorian times and has been a popular spot for visitors to picnic and wander through the woods ever since. Incredibly, the celebrated pre-war rock climber John Menlove Edwards swam down the Linn when its waters were in full spate, a daredevil feat so dangerous that it almost defies belief.

After visiting the Linn, leave the car park in the opposite direction, taking the path marked for Glen Lui to head through the forestry. It shortly crosses a wooden boardwalk to avoid a boggy section before emerging onto a wider track. Turn left here to continue the walk, or you can make a short detour to a waterfall and salmon ladder via the gate opposite.

Along the main route, you'll note some lovely Scots pines on the left with a dense

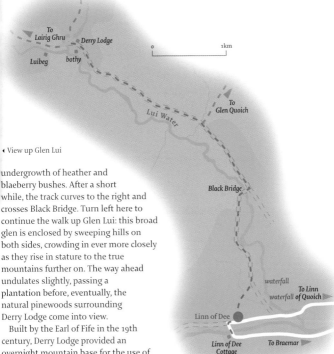

◀ View up Glen Lui

undergrowth of heather and blaeberry bushes. After a short while, the track curves to the right and crosses Black Bridge. Turn left here to continue the walk up Glen Lui: this broad glen is enclosed by sweeping hills on both sides, crowding in ever more closely as they rise in stature to the true mountains further on. The way ahead undulates slightly, passing a plantation before, eventually, the natural pinewoods surrounding Derry Lodge come into view.

Built by the Earl of Fife in the 19th century, Derry Lodge provided an overnight mountain base for the use of shooting parties from the sumptuous Mar Lodge. The impressive listed building, like the rest of the estate, now belongs to the National Trust for Scotland, but is currently boarded up and unused. Nevertheless, this is a magical place to visit, with the old pines, a remnant of the original Caledonian forest that once covered Scotland, stretching northwards into Glen Derry, enclosed by the high Cairngorms. It is worth continuing a short

distance past the lodge to a footbridge, an excellent spot for a picnic. Red deer can often be seen on the far side of the glen.

There is no easy alternative, so the return walk is best made the same way. The views looking back down the glen are very different, giving the distinct impression that you are leaving the wild heartland of the Cairngorms behind.

The Linn of Quoich

Distance 4.5km **Time** 2 hours
Terrain rough woodland paths prone to
flooding, water crossing may be
impassable in spate; track for return
Map OS Explorer OL58
Access no public transport

**Water rages through the rocky Linn of
Quoich, set among the pines at a very
picturesque spot for picnics. Queen
Victoria was once very fond of the Linn
and it became a visitor attraction, but
these days it is much less frequented
than the nearby Linn of Dee.**

The Linn of Quoich is 6km further along
the minor road from the Linn of Dee,
passing the splendid Mar Lodge along the
way. Near the end of the road, just before
the bridge over the Quoich, there is a
parking area on the left (parking charge).

Cross the bridge and take the marked
path on the east side of the river,

following it upstream through the
beautiful remnant of the great Caledonian
pine forest and passing a derelict cottage.

After a short distance you'll come to the
Linn of Quoich. The boarded cottage on
the right was once known as Queen
Victoria's Tea Room and later as the
Princess's Tea Room after Queen Victoria's
granddaughter who married the owner of
Mar Lodge. From the bridge, the Punch
Bowl, a circular pothole where the river
rushes over a slab, can easily be seen
looking upstream. Carved by glacial
meltwater, the bowl gets its name from
its role in local folklore. The Earl of Mar
hosted an enormous hunt here, really as a
pretext to gather the clansmen in advance
of the 1715 Jacobite uprising. Following
the success of the day, gallons of whisky,
boiling water and honey were reputedly
poured into the 'Punch Bowl' and used by
the 2000-strong gathering to toast the

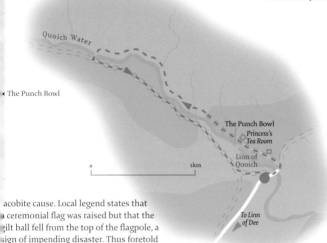

Quoich Water

◄ The Punch Bowl

The Punch Bowl
*Princess's
Tea Room*

Linn of
Quoich

0   1km

To Linn
of Dee

acobite cause. Local legend states that
a ceremonial flag was raised but that the
gilt ball fell from the top of the flagpole, a
sign of impending disaster. Thus foretold
was the defeat of both the 1715 rebellion
and the final destruction of the Jacobites
at Culloden in 1746. The story is made
only marginally less likely by the fact that
the Punch Bowl has a hollow bottom: it
would have been quite a waste of whisky!

Don't cross the bridge, which is a
modern replacement for an original stone
one, but instead continue the walk on the
same side as the 'Tea Room', heading
upstream alongside the river through the
lovely mixed woodland. This stretch,
which passes an attractive waterfall, gives
a real feeling of being in a remote and
hidden glen. As the Scots pines thin out,
there are more open views ahead. Cross a
small feeder stream on stepping stones,
which can be difficult or impassable after
heavy rain, and follow the narrowing path
along the riverbank which has recently
suffered erosion and is tough going in

places, requiring a little clambering on
steep ground.

After a level section, you'll see a wooden
footbridge over the main river. Cross this
and turn left onto a track to begin the
return down the far side of the Quoich,
weaving through some magnificent old
Scots pines on the way; the oldest
specimens are touchingly known as
'grannies'. Where the track emerges from
the trees, there is a good outlook to
Morrone, the high hill rising above
Braemar, topped by a mast. Just beyond,
take a path to the left which drops down
through the woods. This section is steep
but relatively short and soon reaches a
fork at the bottom. Turn left to return to
the bridge at the Linn of Quoich, where
you cross over and head right to retrace
the first part of the walk to the start.

Index